# Python 3 Using ChatGPT / GPT-4

## LICENSE, DISCLAIMER OF LIABILITY, AND LIMITED WARRANTY

By purchasing or using this book and companion files (the "Work"), you agree that this license grants permission to use the contents contained herein, including the disc, but does not give you the right of ownership to any of the textual content in the book / disc or ownership to any of the information or products contained in it. *This license does not permit uploading of the Work onto the Internet or on a network (of any kind) without the written consent of the Publisher.* Duplication or dissemination of any text, code, simulations, images, etc. contained herein is limited to and subject to licensing terms for the respective products, and permission must be obtained from the Publisher or the owner of the content, etc., in order to reproduce or network any portion of the textual material (in any media) that is contained in the Work.

Mercury Learning and Information ("MLI" or "the Publisher") and anyone involved in the creation, writing, or production of the companion disc, accompanying algorithms, code, or computer programs ("the software"), and any accompanying Web site or software of the Work, cannot and do not warrant the performance or results that might be obtained by using the contents of the Work. The author, developers, and the Publisher have used their best efforts to ensure the accuracy and functionality of the textual material and/or programs contained in this package; we, however, make no warranty of any kind, express or implied, regarding the performance of these contents or programs. The Work is sold "as is" without warranty (except for defective materials used in manufacturing the book or due to faulty workmanship).

The author, developers, and the publisher of any accompanying content, and anyone involved in the composition, production, and manufacturing of this work will not be liable for damages of any kind arising out of the use of (or the inability to use) the algorithms, source code, computer programs, or textual material contained in this publication. This includes, but is not limited to, loss of revenue or profit, or other incidental, physical, or consequential damages arising out of the use of this Work.

The sole remedy in the event of a claim of any kind is expressly limited to replacement of the book and/or disc, and only at the discretion of the Publisher. The use of "implied warranty" and certain "exclusions" vary from state to state, and might not apply to the purchaser of this product.

*Companion files for this title are available by writing to the publisher at info@merclearning.com.*

# Python 3 Using ChatGPT / GPT-4

Oswald Campesato

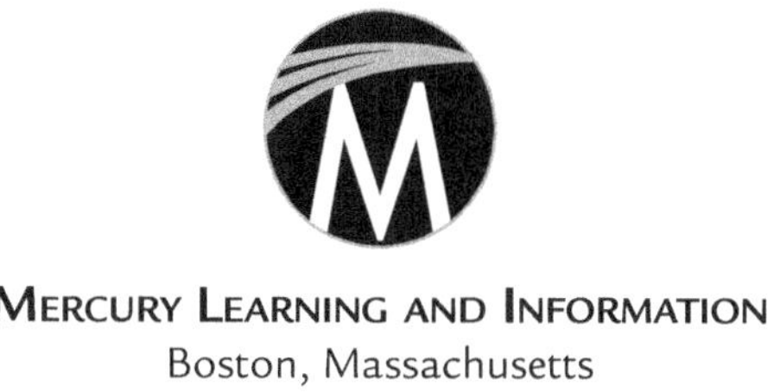

Mercury Learning and Information
Boston, Massachusetts

Publisher: David Pallai
Mercury Learning and Information
121 High Street, 3rd Floor
Boston, MA 02110
info@merclearning.com
www.merclearning.com
800-232-0223

O. Campesato. *Python 3 Using ChatGPT/GPT-4*
ISBN: 978-1-50152-228-4



Library of Congress Control Number: 2023947162
232425321 This book is printed on acid-free paper in the United States of America.

*I'd like to dedicate this book to my parents*
*– may this bring joy and happiness into their lives.*

# CONTENTS

# PREFACE

## WHAT IS THE VALUE PROPOSITION FOR THIS BOOK?

This book starts with an introduction to fundamental aspects of `Python` programming, which include various data types, number formatting, `Unicode` and `UTF-8` handling, and text manipulation techniques. In addition you will learn about loops, conditional logic, and reserved words in `Python`. You will also see how to handle user input, manage exceptions, and work with command-line arguments.

Next, the text transitions to the realm of Generative AI, discussing its distinction from Conversational AI. Popular platforms and models, including ChatGPT, GPT-4, and their competitors, are presented to give readers an understanding of the current AI landscape. The book also sheds light on the capabilities of ChatGPT, its strengths, weaknesses, and potential applications. In addition, you will learn how to generate a variety of `Python` 3 code samples via ChatGPT using the "Advanced Data Analysis" plugin (formerly known as the "Code Interpreter" plugin).

In essence, this book provides a modest bridge between the worlds of `Python` programming and AI, aiming to equip readers with the knowledge and skills to navigate both domains confidently.

## THE TARGET AUDIENCE

This book is intended primarily for people who want to learn both `Python` and how to use ChatGPT with `Python`. This book is also intended to reach an international audience of readers with highly diverse backgrounds in various age groups. In addition, it uses standard English rather than colloquial expressions that might be confusing to those readers. This book provides a comfortable and meaningful learning experience for the intended readers.

## DO I NEED TO LEARN THE THEORY PORTIONS OF THIS BOOK?

The answer depends on the extent to which you plan to become involved in working with ChatGPT and `Python`, perhaps involving LLMs and generative AI. In general, it's probably worthwhile to learn the more theoretical aspects of LLMs that are discussed in this book.

## GETTING THE MOST FROM THIS BOOK

Some people learn well from prose, others learn well from sample code (and large amounts of it), which means that there's no single style that can be used for everyone.

Moreover, some programmers want to run the code first, see what it does, and then return to the code to delve into the details (and others use the opposite approach).

Consequently, there are various types of code samples in this book: some are short, and some are long.

## WHAT DO I NEED TO KNOW FOR THIS BOOK?

Although this book is introductory in nature, some knowledge of `Python` 3.x will certainly be helpful for the code samples. Knowledge of other programming languages (such as `Java`) can also be helpful because of the exposure to programming concepts and constructs. The less technical knowledge that you have, the more diligence will be required in order to understand the various topics that are covered.

If you want to be sure that you can grasp the material in this book, glance through some of the code samples to get an idea of how much is familiar to you and how much is new for you.

## DOES THIS BOOK CONTAIN PRODUCTION-LEVEL CODE SAMPLES?

This book contains basic code samples that are written in `Python`, and their primary purpose is to familiarize you with basic `Python` to help you understand the `Python` code generated via ChatGPT. Moreover, clarity has higher priority than writing more compact code that is more difficult to understand (and possibly more prone to bugs). If you decide to use any of the code in this book, you ought to subject that code to the same rigorous analysis as the other parts of your code base.

## WHAT ARE THE NON-TECHNICAL PREREQUISITES FOR THIS BOOK?

Although the answer to this question is more difficult to quantify, it's especially important to have a strong desire to learn about `NLP`, along with the motivation and discipline to read and understand the code samples. As a reminder, even simple APIs can be a challenge to understand the first time you encounter them, so be prepared to read the code samples several times.

## HOW DO I SET UP A COMMAND SHELL?

If you are a Mac user, there are three ways to do so. The first method is to use `Finder` to navigate to `Applications > Utilities` and then double click on the `Utilities` application. Next, if you already have a command shell available, you can launch a new command shell by typing the following command:

```
open /Applications/Utilities/Terminal.app
```

A second method for Mac users is to open a new command shell on a MacBook from a command shell that is already visible simply by clicking `command+n` in that command shell, and your Mac will launch another command shell.

If you are a PC user, you can install Cygwin (open source *https://cygwin.com/*) that simulates bash commands, or use another toolkit such as MKS (a commercial product). Please read the online documentation that describes the download and installation process. Note that custom aliases are not automatically set if they are defined in a file other than the main start-up file (such as .bash_login).

## COMPANION FILES

All the code samples and figures in this book may be obtained by writing to the publisher at *info@merclearning.com*.

## WHAT ARE THE "NEXT STEPS" AFTER FINISHING THIS BOOK?

The answer to this question varies widely, mainly because the answer depends heavily on your objectives. If you are interested primarily in `NLP`, then you can learn about other LLMs (large language models).

If you are primarily interested in machine learning, there are some subfields of machine learning, such as deep learning and reinforcement learning (and deep reinforcement learning) that might appeal to you. Fortunately, there are many resources available, and you can perform an Internet search for those resources. One other point: the aspects of machine learning for you to learn depend on who you are: the needs of a machine learning engineer, data scientist, manager, student or software developer are all different.

**O. Campesato**
**October 2023**

CHAPTER 1

# INTRODUCTION TO PYTHON 3

This chapter contains an introduction to Python, with information about useful tools for installing Python modules, basic Python constructs, and how to work with some data types in Python.

The first part of this chapter covers how to install Python, some Python environment variables, and how to use the Python interpreter. You will see Python code samples and also how to save Python code in text files that you can launch from the command line. The second part of this chapter shows you how to work with simple data types, such as numbers, fractions, and strings. The final part of this chapter discusses exceptions and how to use them in Python scripts.

**NOTE** *The* Python *files in this book are for* Python *3.x.*

## TOOLS FOR PYTHON

The Anaconda Python distribution is available for Windows, Linux, and Mac, and it's downloadable here: *http://continuum.io/downloads*

Anaconda is well-suited for modules such as numpy and scipy, and if you are a Windows user, Anaconda appears to be a better alternative than working from the command line.

### easy_install and pip

Both easy_install and pip are very easy to use when you need to install Python modules. Whenever you need to install a Python module (and there are many in this book), use either easy_install or pip with the following syntax:

```
easy_install <module-name>
pip install <module-name>
```

**NOTE** *Python-based modules are easier to install than modules with code written in C because they are usually faster. However, they are more difficult in terms of installation.*

## virtualenv

The `virtualenv` tool enables you to create isolated Python environments, and its home page is here: *http://www.virtualenv.org/en/latest/virtualenv.html*

`virtualenv` addresses the problem of preserving the correct dependencies and versions (and indirectly permissions) for different applications. If you are a Python novice, you might not need `virtualenv` right now, but keep this tool in mind.

## IPython

Another very good tool is `IPython` (which won a Jolt award), and its home page is here:

*http://ipython.org/install.html*

Two very nice features of `IPython` are tab expansion and "?," and an example of tab expansion is shown here:

```
$ ipython3
Python 3.9.13 (main, May 24 2022, 21:28:12)
Type 'copyright', 'credits' or 'license' for more information
IPython 8.14.0 -- An enhanced Interactive Python. Type '?' for help.
In [1]:


In [1]: di
%dirs    dict     dir      divmod
```

In the preceding session, if you type the characters `di`, iPython responds with the following line that contains all the functions that start with the letters `di`:

```
%dirs    dict     dir      divmod
```

If you enter a question mark ("?"), `ipython` provides textual assistance, the first part of which is here:

```
IPython -- An enhanced Interactive Python
=========================================

IPython offers a combination of convenient shell
features, special commands and a history mechanism
for both input (command history) and output (results
caching, similar to Mathematica). It is intended to be
a fully compatible replacement for the standard Python
interpreter, while offering vastly improved functionality
and flexibility.
```

The next section shows you how to check whether or not `Python` is installed on your machine, and also where you can download Python.

## PYTHON INSTALLATION

Before you download anything, check if you already have Python installed on your machine (which is likely if you have a Macbook or a Linux machine) by typing the following command in a command shell:

```
python -V
```

The output for the Macbook used in this book is here:

```
Python 3.9.1
```

**NOTE** *Install Python 3.9 (or as close as possible to this version) on your machine so that you will have the same version of* `Python` *that was used to test the* `Python` *files in this book.*

If you need to install `Python` on your machine, navigate to the `Python` home page and select the downloads link or navigate directly to this website:

*http://www.python.org/download/*

In addition, `PythonWin` is available for Windows, and its home page is here:

*http://www.cgl.ucsf.edu/Outreach/pc204/pythonwin.html*

Use any text editor that can create, edit, and save `Python` scripts and save them as plain text files (don't use Microsoft Word).

After you have `Python` installed and configured on your machine, you are ready to work with the `Python` scripts in this book.

## SETTING THE `PATH` ENVIRONMENT VARIABLE (WINDOWS ONLY)

The `PATH` environment variable specifies a list of directories that are searched whenever you specify an executable program from the command line. A very good guide to setting up your environment so that the Python executable is always available in every command shell is to follow the instructions here:

*http://www.blog.pythonlibrary.org/2011/11/24/python-101-setting-up-python-on-windows/*

## LAUNCHING PYTHON ON YOUR MACHINE

There are three different ways to launch Python:

- Use the Python Interactive Interpreter.
- Launch Python scripts from the command line.
- Use an IDE.

The next section shows you how to launch the `Python` interpreter from the command line, and later in this chapter you will learn how to launch `Python` scripts from the command line and also about `Python` IDEs.

**NOTE** *The emphasis in this book is to launch* `Python` *files from the command line or to enter code in the* `Python` *interpreter.*

## The Python Interactive Interpreter

Launch the `Python` interactive interpreter from the command line by opening a command shell and typing the following command:

```
python
```

You will see the following prompt (or something similar):

```
Python 3.9.1 (v3.9.1:1e5d33e9b9, Dec  7 2020, 12:44:01)
[Clang 12.0.0 (clang-1200.0.32.27)] on darwin
Type "help", "copyright", "credits" or "license" for more
information.
>>>
```

Now type the expression `2 + 7` at the prompt:

```
>>> 2 + 7
Python displays the following result:
9
>>>
```

Press `ctrl-d` to exit the `Python` shell.

You can launch any `Python` script from the command line by preceding it with the word "python." For example, if you have a `Python` script `myscript.py` that contains Python commands, launch the script as follows:

```
python myscript.py
```

As a simple illustration, suppose that the `Python` script `myscript.py` contains the following `Python` code:

```
print('Hello World from Python')
print('2 + 7 = ', 2+7)
```

When you launch the preceding `Python` script, you will see the following output:

```
Hello World from Python
2 + 7 =  9
```

## PYTHON IDENTIFIERS

A Python identifier is the name of a variable, function, class, module, or other Python object, and a valid identifier conforms to the following rules:

- It starts with a letter A to Z or a to z or an underscore (_).
- It includes zero or more letters, underscores, and digits (0 to 9).

**NOTE** *Python identifiers cannot contain characters such as @, $, and %.*

Python is a case-sensitive language, so Abc and abc different identifiers in Python.

In addition, Python has the following naming convention:

- Class names start with an uppercase letter and all other identifiers with a lowercase letter.
- An initial underscore is used for private identifiers.
- Two initial underscores are used for strongly private identifiers.

A Python identifier with two initial underscore and two trailing underscore characters indicates a language-defined special name.

## LINES, INDENTATION, AND MULTILINES

Unlike other programming languages (such as Java or Objective-C), Python uses indentation instead of curly braces for code blocks. Indentation must be consistent in a code block, as shown here:

```
if True:
    print("ABC")
    print("DEF")
else:
    print("ABC")
    print("DEF")
```

Multiline statements in Python can terminate with a new line or the backslash ("\") character, as shown here:

```
total = x1 + \
        x2 + \
        x3
```

Obviously you can place x1, x2, and x3 on the same line, so there is no reason to use three separate lines; however, this functionality is available in case you need to add a set of variables that do not fit on a single line.

You can specify multiple statements in one line by using a semicolon (";") to separate each statement, as shown here:

```
a=10; b=5; print(a); print(a+b)
```

The output of the preceding code snippet is here:

```
10
15
```

**NOTE** *The use of semi-colons and the continuation character are discouraged in* `Python`.

## QUOTATION AND COMMENTS IN PYTHON

`Python` allows single (`'`), double (`"`) and triple (`'"` or `"""`) quotes for string literals, provided that they match at the beginning and the end of the string. You can use triple quotes for strings that span multiple lines. The following examples are legal `Python` strings:

```
word  = 'word'
line  = "This is a sentence."
para  = """This is a paragraph. This paragraph contains
more than one sentence."""
```

A string literal that begins with the letter "r" (for "raw") treats everything as a literal character and "escapes" the meaning of meta characters, as shown here:

```
a1 = r'\n'
a2 = r'\r'
a3 = r'\t'
print('a1:',a1,'a2:',a2,'a3:',a3)
```

The output of the preceding code block is here:

```
a1: \n a2: \r a3: \t
```

You can embed a single quote in a pair of double quotes (and vice versa) in order to display a single quote or a double quote. Another way to accomplish the same result is to precede a single or double quote with a backslash ("\") character. The following code block illustrates these techniques:

```
b1 = "'"
b2 = '"'
b3 = '\''
b4 = "\""
print('b1:',b1,'b2:',b2)
print('b3:',b3,'b4:',b4)
```

The output of the preceding code block is here:

```
b1: ' b2: "
b3: ' b4: "
```

A hash sign (#) that is not inside a string literal is the character that indicates the beginning of a comment. Moreover, all characters after the # and up to the physical line end are part of the comment (and ignored by the Python interpreter). Consider the following code block:

```
#!/usr/bin/python
# First comment
print("Hello, Python!")  # second comment
```

This will produce following result:

```
Hello, Python!
```

A comment may be on the same line after a statement or expression:

```
name = "Tom Jones" # This is also comment
```

You can comment multiple lines as follows:

```
# This is comment one
# This is comment two
# This is comment three
```

A blank line in Python is a line containing only white space, a comment, or both.

## SAVING YOUR CODE IN A MODULE

Earlier you saw how to launch the `Python` interpreter from the command line and then enter `Python` commands. However, that everything that you type in the `Python` interpreter is only valid for the current session: if you exit the interpreter and then launch the interpreter again, your previous definitions are no longer valid. Fortunately, `Python` enables you to store code in a text file, as discussed in the next section.

A *module* in `Python` is a text file that contains Python statements. In the previous section, you saw how the `Python` interpreter enables you to test code snippets whose definitions are valid for the current session. If you want to retain the code snippets and other definitions, place them in a text file so that you can execute that code outside of the `Python` interpreter.

The outermost statements in a `Python` are executed from top to bottom when the module is imported for the first time, which will then set up its variables and functions.

A Python module can be run directly from the command line, as shown here:

```
python first.py
```

As an illustration, place the following two statements in a text file called first.py:

```
x = 3
print(x)
```

Now type the following command:

```
python first.py
```

The output from the preceding command is 3, which is the same as executing the preceding code from the Python interpreter.

When a Python module is run directly, the special variable __name__ is set to __main__. You will often see the following type of code in a Python module:

```
if __name__ == '__main__':
    # do something here
    print('Running directly')
```

The preceding code snippet enables Python to determine if a Python module was launched from the command line or imported into another Python module.

## SOME STANDARD MODULES IN PYTHON

The Python Standard Library provides many modules that can simplify your own Python scripts. A list of the Standard Library modules is here:

*http://www.python.org/doc/*

Some of the most important Python modules include cgi, math, os, pickle, random, re, socket, sys, time, and urllib.

The code samples in this book use the modules math, os, random, re, socket, sys, time, and urllib. You need to import these modules in order to use them in your code. For example, the following code block shows you how to import four standard Python modules:

```
import datetime
import re
import sys
import time
```

The code samples in this book import one or more of the preceding modules, as well as other Python modules.

## THE help() AND dir() FUNCTIONS

An internet search for Python-related topics usually returns a number of links with useful information. Alternatively, you can check the official Python documentation site: docs.python.org

In addition, Python provides the help() and dir() functions that are accessible from the Python interpreter. The help() function displays documentation strings, whereas the dir() function displays defined symbols.

For example, if you type help(sys) you will see documentation for the sys module, whereas dir(sys) displays a list of the defined symbols.

Type the following command in the Python interpreter to display the string-related methods in Python:

```
>>> dir(str)
```

The preceding command generates the following output:

```
['__add__', '__class__', '__contains__', '__delattr__',
'__doc__', '__eq__', '__format__', '__ge__',
'__getattribute__', '__getitem__', '__getnewargs__',
'__getslice__', '__gt__', '__hash__', '__init__', '__le__',
'__len__', '__lt__', '__mod__', '__mul__', '__ne__',
'__new__', '__reduce__', '__reduce_ex__', '__repr__',
'__rmod__', '__rmul__', '__setattr__', '__sizeof__',
'__str__', '__subclasshook__', '_formatter_field_name_
split', '_formatter_parser', 'capitalize', 'center',
'count', 'decode', 'encode', 'endswith', 'expandtabs',
'find', 'format', 'index', 'isalnum', 'isalpha', 'isdigit',
'islower', 'isspace', 'istitle', 'isupper', 'join',
'ljust', 'lower', 'lstrip', 'partition', 'replace',
'rfind', 'rindex', 'rjust', 'rpartition', 'rsplit',
'rstrip', 'split', 'splitlines', 'startswith', 'strip',
'swapcase', 'title', 'translate', 'upper', 'zfill']
```

The preceding list gives you a consolidated "dump" of built-in functions (including some that are discussed later in this chapter). Although the max() function obviously returns the maximum value of its arguments, the purpose of other functions such as filter() or map() is not immediately apparent (unless you have used them in other programming languages). In any case, the preceding list provides a starting point for finding out more about various Python built-in functions that are not discussed in this chapter.

Note that while dir() does not list the names of built-in functions and variables, you can obtain this information from the standard module __builtin__ that is automatically imported under the name __builtins__:

```
>>> dir(__builtins__)
```

The following command shows you how to get more information about a function:

```
help(str.lower)
```

The output from the preceding command is here:

```
Help on method_descriptor:

lower(...)
    S.lower() -> string

    Return a copy of the string S converted to lowercase.
(END)
```

Check the online documentation and also experiment with `help()` and `dir()` when you need additional information about a particular function or module.

## COMPILE TIME AND RUNTIME CODE CHECKING

`Python` performs some compile-time checking, but most checks (including type, name, and so forth) are *deferred* until code execution. Consequently, if your `Python` code references a user-defined function that that does not exist, the code will compile successfully. In fact, the code will fail with an exception *only* when the code execution path references the nonexistent function.

As a simple example, consider the following `Python` function `myFunc` that references the nonexistent function called `DoesNotExist`:

```
def myFunc(x):
    if x == 3:
        print(DoesNotExist(x))
    else:
        print('x: ',x)
```

The preceding code will only fail when the `myFunc` function is passed the value 3, after which `Python` raises an error.

In Chapter 2, you will learn how to define and invoke user-defined functions, along with an explanation of the difference between local versus global variables in `Python`.

Now that you understand some basic concepts (such as how to use the Python interpreter) and how to launch your custom `Python` modules, the next section discusses primitive data types in Python.

## SIMPLE DATA TYPES IN PYTHON

`Python` supports primitive data types, such as numbers (integers, floating point numbers, and exponential numbers), strings, and dates. `Python` also supports more complex data types, such as lists (or arrays), tuples, and dictionaries, all of which are discussed in Chapter 3. The next several sections discuss some of the `Python` primitive data types, along with code snippets that show you how to perform various operations on those data types.

## WORKING WITH NUMBERS

`Python` provides arithmetic operations for manipulating numbers a straightforward manner that is similar to other programming languages. The following examples involve arithmetic operations on integers:

```
>>> 2+2
4
>>> 4/3
1
>>> 3*8
24
```

The following example assigns numbers to two variables and computes their product:

```
>>> x = 4
>>> y = 7
>>> x * y
28
```

The following examples demonstrate arithmetic operations involving integers:

```
>>> 2+2
4
>>> 4/3
1
>>> 3*8
24
```

Notice that division ("/") of two integers is actually truncation in which only the integer result is retained. The following example converts a floating point number into exponential form:

```
>>> fnum = 0.00012345689000007
>>> "%.14e"%fnum
'1.23456890000070e-04'
```

You can use the `int()` function and the `float()` function to convert strings to numbers:

```
word1 = "123"
word2 = "456.78"
var1 = int(word1)
var2 = float(word2)
print("var1: ",var1," var2: ",var2)
```

The output from the preceding code block is here:

```
var1:  123  var2:  456.78
```

Alternatively, you can use the `eval()` function:

```
word1 = "123"
word2 = "456.78"
var1 = eval(word1)
var2 = eval(word2)
print("var1: ",var1," var2: ",var2)
```

If you attempt to convert a string that is not a valid integer or a floating point number, `Python` raises an exception, so it's advisable to place your code in a `try/except` block (discussed later in this chapter).

## Working With Other Bases

Numbers in `Python` are in base 10 (the default), but you can easily convert numbers to other bases. For example, the following code block initializes the variable `x` with the value `1234`, and then displays that number in base `2`, `8`, and `16`, respectively:

```
>>> x = 1234
>>> bin(x) '0b10011010010'
>>> oct(x) '0o2322'
>>> hex(x) '0x4d2' >>>
```

Use the `format()` function if you wan to suppress the `0b`, `0o`, or `0x` prefixes, as shown here:

```
>>> format(x, 'b') '10011010010'
>>> format(x, 'o') '2322'
>>> format(x, 'x') '4d2'
```

Negative integers are displayed with a negative sign:

```
>>> x = -1234
>>> format(x, 'b') '-10011010010'
>>> format(x, 'x') '-4d2'
```

## The `chr()` Function

The `Python chr()` function takes a positive integer as a parameter and converts it to its corresponding alphabetic value (if one exists). The letters A through Z have decimal representation of `65` through `91` (which corresponds to hexadecimal `41` through `5b`), and the lowercase letters `a` through `z` have decimal representation `97` through `122` (hexadecimal `61` through `7b`).

Here is an example of using the `chr()` function to print uppercase `A`:

```
>>> x=chr(65)
>>> x
'A'
```

The following code block prints the ASCII values for a range of integers:

```
result = ""
for x in range(65,91):
  print(x, chr(x))
  result = result+chr(x)+' '
print("result: ",result)
```

**NOTE** Python *2 uses* ASCII *strings whereas* Python *3 uses* UTF-8.

You can represent a range of characters with the following line:

```
for x in range(65,91):
```

However, the following equivalent code snippet is more intuitive:

```
for x in range(ord('A'), ord('Z')):
```

If you want to display the result for lowercase letters, change the preceding range from (65,91) to either of the following statements:

```
for x in range(65,91):
for x in range(ord('a'), ord('z')):
```

## The round() Function in Python

The Python round() function enables you to round decimal values to the nearest precision:

```
>>> round(1.23, 1)
1.2
>>> round(-3.42,1)
-3.4
```

## Formatting Numbers in Python

Python allows you to specify the number of decimal places of precision to use when printing decimal numbers, as shown here:

```
>>> x = 1.23456
>>> format(x, '0.2f')
'1.23'
>>> format(x, '0.3f')
'1.235'
>>> 'value is {:0.3f}'.format(x) 'value is 1.235'
>>> from decimal import Decimal
>>> a = Decimal('4.2')
>>> b = Decimal('2.1')
>>> a + b
Decimal('6.3')
>>> print(a + b)
6.3
>>> (a + b) == Decimal('6.3')
True
```

```
>>> x = 1234.56789
>>> # Two decimal places of accuracy
>>> format(x, '0.2f')
'1234.57'
>>> # Right justified in 10 chars, one-digit accuracy
>>> format(x, '>10.1f')
' 1234.6'
>>> # Left justified
>>> format(x, '<10.1f') '1234.6 '
>>> # Centered
>>> format(x, '^10.1f') ' 1234.6 '
>>> # Inclusion of thousands separator
>>> format(x, ',')
'1,234.56789'
>>> format(x, '0,.1f')
'1,234.6'
```

## WORKING WITH FRACTIONS

Python supports the Fraction() function (which is define in the fractions module) that accepts two integers that represent the numerator and the denominator (which must be nonzero) of a fraction. Several example of defining and manipulating fractions in Python are shown here:

```
>>> from fractions import Fraction
>>> a = Fraction(5, 4)
>>> b = Fraction(7, 16)
>>> print(a + b)
27/16
>>> print(a * b) 35/64
>>> # Getting numerator/denominator
>>> c = a * b
>>> c.numerator
35
>>> c.denominator 64
>>> # Converting to a float >>> float(c)
0.546875
>>> # Limiting the denominator of a value
>>> print(c.limit_denominator(8))
4
>>> # Converting a float to a fraction >>> x = 3.75
>>> y = Fraction(*x.as_integer_ratio())
>>> y
Fraction(15, 4)
```

Before delving into Python code samples that work with strings, the next section briefly discusses Unicode and UTF-8, both of which are character encodings.

## UNICODE AND UTF-8

A Unicode string consists of a sequence of numbers that are between 0 and 0x10ffff, where each number represents a group of bytes. An encoding is the manner in which a Unicode string is translated into a sequence of bytes.

Among the various encodings, UTF-8 ("Unicode transformation format") is perhaps the most common, and it's also the default encoding for many systems. The digit 8 in UTF-8 indicates that the encoding uses 8-bit numbers, whereas UTF-16 uses 16-bit numbers (but this encoding is less common).

The ASCII character set is a subset of UTF-8, so a valid ASCII string can be read as a UTF-8 string without any re-encoding required. In addition, a Unicode string can be converted into a UTF-8 string.

## WORKING WITH UNICODE

Python supports Unicode, which means that you can render characters in different languages. Unicode data can be stored and manipulated in the same way as strings. Create a Unicode string by prepending the letter 'u', as shown here:

```
>>> u'Hello from Python!'
u'Hello from Python!'
```

Special characters can be included in a string by specifying their Unicode value. For example, the following Unicode string embeds a space (which has the Unicode value 0x0020) in a string:

```
>>> u'Hello\u0020from Python!'
u'Hello from Python!'
```

Listing 1.1 displays the contents of unicode1.py that illustrates how to display a string of characters in Japanese and another string of characters in Chinese (Mandarin).

***LISTING 1.1: unicode1.py***

```
chinese1 = u'\u5c07\u63a2\u8a0e HTML5 \u53ca\u5176\u4ed6'
hiragana = u'D3 \u306F \u304B\u3063\u3053\u3043\u3043 \u3067\u3059!'

print('Chinese:',chinese1)
print('Hiragana:',hiragana)
```

The output of Listing 1.2 is here:

```
Chinese: 將探討 HTML5 及其他
Hiragana: D3 は かっこぃぃ です!
```

The next portion of this chapter shows you how to "slice and dice" text strings with built-in Python functions.

## WORKING WITH STRINGS

You can concatenate two strings using the '+' operator. The following example prints a string and then concatenates two single-letter strings:

```
>>> 'abc'
'abc'
```

```
>>> 'a' + 'b'
'ab'
```

You can use "+" or "*" to concatenate identical strings, as shown here:

```
>>> 'a' + 'a' + 'a'
'aaa'
>>> 'a' * 3
'aaa'
```

You can assign strings to variables and print them using the `print()` command:

```
>>> print('abc')
abc
>>> x = 'abc'
>>> print(x)
abc
>>> y = 'def'
>>> print(x + y)
abcdef
```

You can "unpack" the letters of a string and assign them to variables, as shown here:

```
>>> str = "World"
>>> x1,x2,x3,x4,x5 = str
>>> x1
'W'
>>> x2
'o'
>>> x3
'r'
>>> x4
'l'
>>> x5
'd'
```

The preceding code snippets shows you how easy it is to extract the letters in a text string, and in Chapter 3 you will learn how to "unpack" other `Python` data structures.

You can extract substrings of a string as shown in the following examples:

```
>>> x = "abcdef"
>>> x[0]
'a'
>>> x[-1]
'f'
>>> x[1:3]
'bc'
>>> x[0:2] + x[5:]
'abf'
```

However, you will cause an error if you attempt to "subtract" two strings, as you probably expect:

```
>>> 'a' - 'b'
Traceback (most recent call last):
  File "<stdin>", line 1, in <module>
TypeError: unsupported operand type(s) for -: 'str' and 'str'
```

The `try/except` construct in `Python` (discussed later in this chapter) enables you to handle the preceding type of exception more gracefully.

## Comparing Strings

You can use the methods `lower()` and `upper()` to convert a string to lowercase and uppercase, respectively, as shown here:

```
>>> 'Python'.lower()
'python'
>>> 'Python'.upper()
'PYTHON'
>>>
```

The methods `lower()` and `upper()` are useful for performing a case insensitive comparison of two `ASCII` strings. Listing 1.2 displays the contents of `compare.py` that uses the `lower()` function in order to compare two `ASCII` strings.

***LISTING 1.2: compare.py***

```
x = 'Abc'
y = 'abc'

if(x == y):
  print('x and y: identical')
elif (x.lower() == y.lower()):
  print('x and y: case insensitive match')
else:
  print('x and y: different')
```

Since `x` contains mixed case letters and `y` contains lowercase letters, Listing 1.2 displays the following output:

```
x and y: different
```

## Formatting Strings in Python

`Python` provides the functions `string.lstring()`, `string.rstring()`, and `string.center()` for positioning a text string so that it is left-justified, right-justified, and centered, respectively. As you saw in a previous section, `Python` also provides the `format()` method for advanced interpolation features.

Now enter the following commands in the Python interpreter:

```
import string

str1 = 'this is a string'
print(string.ljust(str1, 10))
print(string.rjust(str1, 40))
print(string.center(str1,40))
```

The output is shown here:

```
this is a string
                        this is a string
            this is a string
```

The next portion of this chapter shows you how to "slice and dice" text strings with built-in Python functions.

## SLICING AND SPLICING STRINGS

Python enables you to extract substrings of a string (called "slicing") using array notation. Slice notation is `start:stop:step`, where the start, stop, and step values are integers that specify the start value, end value, and the increment value. The interesting part about slicing in Python is that you can use the value `-1`, which operates from the right side of a string instead of the left side of a string.

Some examples of slicing a string are here:

```
text1 = "this is a string"
print('First 7 characters:',text1[0:7])
print('Characters 2-4:',text1[2:4])
print('Right-most character:',text1[-1])
print('Right-most 2 characters:',text1[-3:-1])
```

The output from the preceding code block is here:

```
First 7 characters: this is
Characters 2-4: is
Right-most character: g
Right-most 2 characters: in
```

Later in this chapter you will see how to insert a string in the middle of another string.

### Testing for Digits and Alphabetic Characters

Python enables you to examine each character in a string and then test whether that character is a bona fide digit or an alphabetic character. This section provides a precursor to regular expressions that are discussed in Chapter 4.

Listing 1.3 displays the contents of `char_types.py` that illustrates how to determine if a string contains digits or characters. In case you are unfamiliar with the conditional "if" statement in Listing 1.3, more detailed information is available in Chapter 2.

***LISTING 1.3: char_types.py***

```
str1 = "4"
str2 = "4234"
str3 = "b"
str4 = "abc"
str5 = "a1b2c3"

if(str1.isdigit()):
  print("this is a digit:",str1)

if(str2.isdigit()):
  print("this is a digit:",str2)

if(str3.isalpha()):
  print("this is alphabetic:",str3)

if(str4.isalpha()):
  print("this is alphabetic:",str4)

if(not str5.isalpha()):
  print("this is not pure alphabetic:",str5)

print("capitalized first letter:",str5.title())
```

Listing 1.3 initializes some variables, followed by 2 conditional tests that check whether or not `str1` and `str2` are digits using the `isdigit()` function. The next portion of Listing 1.3 checks if `str3`, `str4`, and `str5` are alphabetic strings using the `isalpha()` function. The output of Listing 1.3 is here:

```
this is a digit: 4
this is a digit: 4234
this is alphabetic: b
this is alphabetic: abc
this is not pure alphabetic: a1b2c3
capitalized first letter: A1B2C3
```

## SEARCH AND REPLACE A STRING IN OTHER STRINGS

`Python` provides methods for searching and also for replacing a string in a second text string. Listing 1.4 displays the contents of `find_pos1.py` that shows you how to use the find function to search for the occurrence of one string in another string.

***LISTING 1.4: find_pos1.py***

```
item1 = 'abc'
item2 = 'Abc'
text = 'This is a text string with abc'
```

```
pos1 = text.find(item1)
pos2 = text.find(item2)

print('pos1=',pos1)
print('pos2=',pos2)
```

Listing 1.4 initializes the variables `item1`, `item2`, and `text`, and then searches for the index of the contents of `item1` and `item2` in the string text. The `Python` `find()` function returns the column number where the first successful match occurs; otherwise, the `find()` function returns a `-1` if a match is unsuccessful.

The output from launching Listing 1.4 is here:

```
pos1= 27
pos2= -1
```

In addition to the `find()` method, you can use the `in` operator when you want to test for the presence of an element, as shown here:

```
>>> lst = [1,2,3]
>>> 1 in lst
True
```

Listing 1.5 displays the contents of `replace1.py` that shows you how to replace one string with another string.

***LISTING 1.5: replace1.py***

```
text = 'This is a text string with abc'
print('text:',text)
text = text.replace('is a', 'was a')
print('text:',text)
```

Listing 1.5 starts by initializing the variable text and then printing its contents. The next portion of Listing 1.5 replaces the occurrence of "is a" with "was a" in the string text, and then prints the modified string. The output from launching Listing 1.5 is here:

```
text: This is a text string with abc
text: This was a text string with abc
```

## REMOVE LEADING AND TRAILING CHARACTERS

`Python` provides the functions `strip()`, `lstrip()`, and `rstrip()` to remove characters in a text string. Listing 1.6 displays the contents of `remove1.py` that shows you how to search for a string.

***LISTING 1.6: remove1.py***

```
text = '   leading and trailing white space    '
print('text1:','x',text,'y')
```

```
text = text.lstrip()
print('text2:','x',text,'y')

text = text.rstrip()
print('text3:','x',text,'y')
```

Listing 1.6 starts by concatenating the letter x and the contents of the variable text, and then printing the result. The second part of Listing 1.6 removes the leading white spaces in the string text and then appends the result to the letter x. The third part of Listing 1.6 removes the trailing white spaces in the string text (note that the leading white spaces have already been removed) and then appends the result to the letter x.

The output from launching Listing 1.6 is here:

```
text1: x    leading and trailing white space    y
text2: x leading and trailing white space    y
text3: x leading and trailing white space y
```

If you want to remove extra white spaces inside a text string, use the replace() function as discussed in the previous section. The following example illustrates how this can be accomplished, which also contains the re module as a "preview" for what you will learn in Chapter 4:

```
import re
text = 'a    b'
a = text.replace(' ', '')
b = re.sub('\s+', ' ', text)

print(a)
print(b)
```

The result is here:

```
ab
a b
```

Chapter 2 shows you how to use the join() function in order to remove extra white spaces in a text string.

## PRINTING TEXT WITHOUT NEWLINE CHARACTERS

If you need to suppress white space and a newline between objects output with multiple print() statements, you can use concatenation or the write() function.

The first technique is to concatenate the string representations of each object using the str() function prior to printing the result. For example, run the following statement in Python:

```
x = str(9)+str(0xff)+str(-3.1)
print('x: ',x)
```

The output is shown here:

```
x:  9255-3.1
```

The preceding line contains the concatenation of the numbers `9` and `255` (which is the decimal value of the hexadecimal number `0xff`) and `-3.1`.

Incidentally, you can use the `str()` function with modules and user-defined classes. An example involving the Python built-in module `sys` is here:

```
>>> import sys
>>> print(str(sys))
<module 'sys' (built-in)>
```

The following code snippet illustrates how to use the `write()` function to display a string:

```
import sys
write = sys.stdout.write
write('123')
write('123456789')
```

The output is here:

```
123123456789
```

## TEXT ALIGNMENT

`Python` provides the methods `ljust()`, `rjust()`, and `center()` for aligning text. The `ljust()` and `rjust()` functions left justify and right justify a text string, respectively, whereas the `center()` function will center a string. An example is shown in the following code block:

```
text = 'Hello World'
text.ljust(20)
'Hello World '
>>> text.rjust(20)
' Hello World'
>>> text.center(20)
' Hello World '
```

You can use the `Python format()` function to align text. Use the <, >, `or` ^ characters, along with a desired width, in order to right justify, left justify, and center the text, respectively. The following examples illustrate how you can specify text justification:

```
>>> format(text, '>20')
'         Hello World'
>>>
>>> format(text, '<20')
'Hello World         '
```

```
>>>
>>> format(text, '^20')
'    Hello World     '
>>>
```

## WORKING WITH DATES

Python provides a rich set of date-related functions. Listing 1.7 displays the contents of the Python script date_time2.py that displays various date-related values, such as the current date and time; the day of the week, month, and year; and the time in seconds since the epoch.

***LISTING 1.7: date_time2.py***

```
import time
import datetime

print("Time in seconds since the epoch: %s" %time.time())
print("Current date and time: " , datetime.datetime.now())
print("Or like this: " ,datetime.datetime.now().
strftime("%y-%m-%d-%H-%M"))

print("Current year: ", datetime.date.today().
strftime("%Y"))
print("Month of year: ", datetime.date.today().
strftime("%B"))
print("Week number of the year: ", datetime.date.today().
strftime("%W"))
print("Weekday of the week: ", datetime.date.today().
strftime("%w"))
print("Day of year: ", datetime.date.today().
strftime("%j"))
print("Day of the month : ", datetime.date.today().
strftime("%d"))
print("Day of week: ", datetime.date.today().
strftime("%A"))
```

Listing 1.8 displays the output generated by running the code in Listing 1.7.

***LISTING 1.8 datetime2.out***

```
Time in seconds since the epoch: 1375144195.66
Current date and time:  2013-07-29 17:29:55.664164
Or like this:  13-07-29-17-29
Current year:  2013
Month of year:  July
Week number of the year:  30
Weekday of the week:  1
Day of year:  210
Day of the month :  29
Day of week:  Monday
```

Python also enables you to perform arithmetic calculates with date-related values, as shown in the following code block:

```
>>> from datetime import timedelta
>>> a = timedelta(days=2, hours=6)
>>> b = timedelta(hours=4.5)
>>> c = a + b
>>> c.days
2
>>> c.seconds
37800
>>> c.seconds / 3600
10.5
>>> c.total_seconds() / 3600
58.5
```

## Converting Strings to Dates

Listing 1.9 displays the contents of string2date.py that illustrates how to convert a string to a date, and also how to calculate the difference between two dates.

***LISTING 1.9: string2date.py***

```
from datetime import datetime

text = '2024-08-13'
y = datetime.strptime(text, '%Y-%m-%d')
z = datetime.now()
diff = z - y
print('Date difference:',diff)
```

The output from Listing 1.9 is shown here:

```
Date difference: -210 days, 18:58:40.197130
```

## EXCEPTION HANDLING IN PYTHON

Unlike JavaScript you cannot add a number and a string in Python. However, you can detect an illegal operation using the try/except construct in Python, which is similar to the try/catch construct in languages such as JavaScript and Java.

An example of a try/except block is here:

```
try:
  x = 4
  y = 'abc'
  z = x + y
except:
  print 'cannot add incompatible types:', x, y
```

When you run the preceding code in `Python`, the `print()` statement in the `except` code block is executed because the variables `x` and `y` have incompatible types.

Earlier in the chapter you also saw that subtracting two strings throws an exception:

```
>>> 'a' - 'b'
Traceback (most recent call last):
  File "<stdin>", line 1, in <module>
TypeError: unsupported operand type(s) for -: 'str' and 'str'
```

A simple way to handle this situation is to use a `try/except` block:

```
>>> try:
...   print('a' - 'b')
... except TypeError:
...   print('TypeError exception while trying to subtract two strings')
... except:
...   print('Exception while trying to subtract two strings')
...
```

The output from the preceding code block is here:

```
TypeError exception while trying to subtract two strings
```

As you can see, the preceding code block specifies the finer-grained exception called `TypeError`, followed by a generic `except` code block to handle all other exceptions that might occur during the execution of your `Python` code. This style is similar to the exception handling in Java code.

Listing 1.10 displays the contents of `exception1.py` that illustrates how to handle various types of exceptions.

***LISTING 1.10: exception1.py***

```
import sys

try:
    f = open('myfile.txt')
    s = f.readline()
    i = int(s.strip())
except IOError as err:
    print("I/O error: {0}".format(err))
except ValueError:
    print("Could not convert data to an integer.")
except:
    print("Unexpected error:", sys.exc_info()[0])
    raise
```

Listing 1.10 contains a `try` block followed by three `except` statements. If an error occurs in the `try` block, the first `except` statement is compared with the type of exception that occurred. If there is a match, then the subsequent print() statement is executed, and the program terminates. If not, a similar test is performed with the second except statement. If neither except statement matches the exception, the third except statement handles the exception, which involves printing a message and then "raising" an exception. Note that you can also specify multiple exception types in a single statement, as shown here:

```
except (NameError, RuntimeError, TypeError):
    print('One of three error types occurred')
```

The preceding code block is more compact, but you do not know which of the three error types occurred. Python allows you to define custom exceptions, but this topic is beyond the scope of this book.

## HANDLING USER INPUT

Python enables you to read user input from the command line via the input() function or the raw_input() function. Typically you assign user input to a variable, which will contain all characters that users enter from the keyboard. User input terminates when users press the <return> key (which is included with the input characters). Listing 1.11 displays the contents of user_input1.py that prompts users for their name and then uses interpolation to display a response.

***LISTING 1.11: user_input1.py***

```
userInput = input("Enter your name: ")
print ("Hello %s, my name is Python" % userInput)
```

The output of Listing 1.11 is here (assume that the user entered the word "Dave"):

```
Hello Dave, my name is Python
```

The print() statement in Listing 1.11 uses string interpolation via %s, which substitutes the value of the variable after the % symbol. This functionality is obviously useful when you want to specify something that is determined at run-time.

User input can cause exceptions (depending on the operations that your code performs), so it's important to include exception-handling code.

Listing 1.12 displays the contents of user_input2.py that prompts users for a string and attempts to convert the string to a number in a try/except block.

***LISTING 1.12: user_input2.py***

```
userInput = input("Enter something: ")

try:
  x = 0 + eval(userInput)
```

```
  print('you entered the number:',userInput)
except:
  print(userInput,'is a string')
```

Listing 1.12 adds the number `0` to the result of converting a user's input to a number. If the conversion was successful, a message with the user's input is displayed. If the conversion failed, the `except` code block consists of a `print` statement that displays a message.

**NOTE** *This code sample uses the* `eval()` *function, which should be avoided so that your code does not evaluate arbitrary (and possibly destructive) commands.*

Listing 1.13 displays the contents of `user_input3.py` that prompts users for two numbers and attempts to compute their sum in a pair of `try/except` blocks.

***LISTING 1.13: user_input3.py***

```
sum = 0

msg = 'Enter a number:'
val1 = input(msg)

try:
  sum = sum + eval(val1)
except:
  print(val1,'is a string')

msg = 'Enter a number:'
val2 = input(msg)

try:
  sum = sum + eval(val2)
except:
  print(val2,'is a string')

print('The sum of',val1,'and',val2,'is',sum)
```

Listing 1.13 contains two `try` blocks, each of which is followed by an `except` statement. The first `try` block attempts to add the first user-supplied number to the variable `sum`, and the second `try` block attempts to add the second user-supplied number to the previously entered number. An error message occurs if either input string is not a valid number; if both are valid numbers, a message is displayed containing the input numbers and their sum. Be sure to read the caveat regarding the `eval()` function that is mentioned earlier in this chapter.

## COMMAND-LINE ARGUMENTS

`Python` provides a `getopt` module to parse command-line options and arguments, and the `Python sys` module provides access to any command-line arguments via the `sys.argv`. This serves two purposes:

1. `sys.argv` is the list of command-line arguments.
2. `len(sys.argv)` is the number of command-line arguments.

Here `sys.argv[0]` is the program name, so if the `Python` program is called `test.py`, it matches the value of `sys.argv[0]`.

Now you can provide input values for a `Python` program on the command line instead of providing input values by prompting users for their input.

As an example, consider the script `test.py` shown here:

```
#!/usr/bin/python
import sys
print('Number of arguments:',len(sys.argv),'arguments')
print('Argument List:', str(sys.argv))
```

Now run above script as follows:

```
python test.py arg1 arg2 arg3
```

This will produce following result:

```
Number of arguments: 4 arguments.
Argument List: ['test.py', 'arg1', 'arg2', 'arg3']
```

The ability to specify input values from the command line provides useful functionality. For example, suppose that you have a custom Python class that contains the methods `add` and `subtract` to add and subtract a pair of numbers.

You can use command-line arguments in order to specify which method to execute on a pair of numbers, as shown here:

```
python MyClass add 3 5
python MyClass subtract 3 5
```

This functionality is very useful because you can programmatically execute different methods in a Python class, which means that you can write unit tests for your code as well. Read Chapter 8 to learn how to create custom Python classes.

Listing 1.14 displays the contents of `hello.py` that shows you how to use `sys.argv` to check the number of command line parameters.

***LISTING 1.14: hello.py***

```
import sys

def main():
  if len(sys.argv) >= 2:
    name = sys.argv[1]
  else:
    name = 'World'
  print('Hello', name)
```

```
# Standard boilerplate to invoke the main() function
if __name__ == '__main__':
  main()
```

Listing 1.14 defines the `main()` function that checks the number of command-line parameters: if this value is at least `2`, then the variable `name` is assigned the value of the second parameter (the first parameter is `hello.py`), otherwise `name` is assigned the value `Hello`. The `print()` statement then prints the value of the variable `name`.

The final portion of Listing 1.14 uses conditional logic to determine whether or not to execute the `main()` function.

## SUMMARY

This chapter showed you how to work with numbers and perform arithmetic operations on numbers, and then you learned how to work with strings and use string operations. You also learned how to use the try/except construct to handle exceptions that might occur in your `Python` code. The next chapter shows you how to work with conditional statements, loops, and user-defined functions in `Python`.

CHAPTER 2

# Conditional Logic, Loops, and Functions

This chapter introduces you to various ways to perform conditional logic in `Python`, as well as control structures and user-defined functions in Python. Virtually every `Python` program that performs useful calculations requires some type of conditional logic or control structure (or both). Although the syntax for these Python features is slightly different from other languages, the functionality will be familiar to you.

The first part of this chapter contains code samples that illustrate how to handle `if-else` conditional logic in Python, as well as `if-elsif-else` statements. The second part of this chapter discusses loops and while statements in `Python`. This section contains an assortment of examples (comparing strings, computing numbers raised to different exponents, and so forth) that illustrate various ways that you can use loops and while statements in `Python`.

The third part of this chapter contains examples that involve nested loops and recursion. The final part of this chapter introduces you to user-defined `Python` functions.

## PRECEDENCE OF OPERATORS IN PYTHON

When you have an expression involving numbers, you might remember that multiplication ("*") and division ("/") have higher precedence than addition ("+") or subtraction ("–"). Exponentiation has even higher precedence than these four arithmetic operators.

However, instead of relying on precedence rules, it's simpler (as well as safer) to use parentheses. For example, `(x/y)+10` is clearer than `x/y+10`, even though they are equivalent expressions.

As another example, the following two arithmetic expressions are equivalent, but the second is less error prone than the first:

```
x/y+3*z/8+x*y/z-3*x
(x/y)+(3*z)/8+(x*y)/z-(3*x)
```

In any case, the following website contains precedence rules for operators in Python:

*http://www.mathcs.emory.edu/~valerie/courses/fall10/155/resources/op_precedence.html*

## PYTHON RESERVED WORDS

Every programming language has a set of reserved words, which is a set of words that cannot be used as identifiers, and Python is no exception. The Python reserved words are: and, exec, not, assert, finally, or, break, for, pass, class, from, print, continue, global, raise, def, if, return, del, import, try, elif, in, while, else, is, with, except, lambda, and yield.

If you inadvertently use a reserved word as a variable, you will see an "invalid syntax" error message instead of a "reserved word" error message. For example, suppose you create a Python script test1.py with the following code:

```
break = 2
print('break =', break)
```

If you run the preceding Python code you will see the following output:

```
  File "test1.py", line 2
    break = 2
          ^
SyntaxError: invalid syntax
```

However, a quick inspection of the Python code reveals the fact that you are attempting to use the reserved word break as a variable.

## WORKING WITH LOOPS IN PYTHON

Python supports for loops, while loops, and range() statements. The following subsections illustrate how you can use each of these constructs.

### Python for Loops

Python supports the for loop whose syntax is slightly different from other languages (such as JavaScript and Java). The following code block shows you how to use a for loop in Python in order to iterate through the elements in a list:

```
>>> x = ['a', 'b', 'c']
>>> for w in x:
...    print(w)
...
a
b
c
```

The preceding code snippet prints three letters on three separate lines. You can force the output to be displayed on the same line (which will "wrap" if you specify a large enough number of characters) by appending a comma "," in the print statement, as shown here:

```
>>> x = ['a', 'b', 'c']
>>> for w in x:
...   print(w, end=' ')
...
a b c
```

You can use this type of code when you want to display the contents of a text file in a single line instead of multiple lines.

`Python` also provides the built-in `reversed()` function that reverses the direction of the loop, as shown here:

```
>>> a = [1, 2, 3, 4, 5]
>>> for x in reversed(a):
... print(x)
5
4
3
2
1
```

Note that reversed iteration only works if the size of the current object can be determined or if the object implements a `__reversed__()` special method.

## A `for` Loop with `try/except` in Python

Listing 2.1 displays the contents of `StringToNums.py` that illustrates how to calculate the sum of a set of integers that have been converted from strings.

***LISTING 2.1: StringToNums.py***

```
line = '1 2 3 4 10e abc'
sum  = 0
invalidStr = ""

print('String of numbers:',line)

for str in line.split(" "):
  try:
    sum = sum + eval(str)
  except:
    invalidStr = invalidStr + str + ' '

print('sum:', sum)
if(invalidStr != ""):
  print('Invalid strings:',invalidStr)
else:
  print('All substrings are valid numbers')
```

Listing 2.1 initializes the variables `line, sum, and invalidStr`, and then displays the contents of line. The next portion of Listing 2.1 splits the contents of `line` into words, and then uses a `try` block in order to add the numeric value of each word to the variable sum. If an exception occurs, the contents of the current `str` is appended to the variable `invalidStr`.

When the loop has finished execution, Listing 2.1 displays the sum of the numeric words, followed by the list of words that are not numbers. The output from Listing 2.1 is here:

```
String of numbers: 1 2 3 4 10e abc
sum: 10
Invalid strings: 10e abc
```

## Numeric Exponents in Python

Listing 2.2 displays the contents of `Nth_exponent.py` that illustrates how to calculate intermediate powers of a set of integers.

***LISTING 2.2: Nth_exponent.py***

```
maxPower = 4
maxCount = 4

def pwr(num):
  prod = 1
  for n in range(1,maxPower+1):
    prod = prod*num
    print(num,'to the power',n, 'equals',prod)
  print('-----------')

for num in range(1,maxCount+1):
    pwr(num)
```

Listing 2.2 contains a function called `pwr()` that accepts a numeric value. This function contains a loop that prints the value of that number raised to the power n, where n ranges between `1` and `maxPower+1`.

The second part of Listing 2.2 contains a `for` loop that invokes the function `pwr()` with the numbers between `1` and `maxPower+1`. The output from Listing 2.2 is here:

```
1 to the power 1 equals 1
1 to the power 2 equals 1
1 to the power 3 equals 1
1 to the power 4 equals 1
-----------
2 to the power 1 equals 2
2 to the power 2 equals 4
2 to the power 3 equals 8
2 to the power 4 equals 16
-----------
```

```
3 to the power 1 equals 3
3 to the power 2 equals 9
3 to the power 3 equals 27
3 to the power 4 equals 81
-----------
4 to the power 1 equals 4
4 to the power 2 equals 16
4 to the power 3 equals 64
4 to the power 4 equals 256
-----------
```

## NESTED LOOPS

Listing 2.3 displays the contents of `Triangular1.py` that illustrates how to print a row of consecutive integers (starting from `1`), where the length of each row is one greater than the previous row.

***LISTING 2.3: Triangular1.py***

```
max = 8
for x in range(1,max+1):
  for y in range(1,x+1):
    print(y, '', end='')
  print()
```

Listing 2.3 initializes the variable `max` with the value 8, followed by an outer `for` loop whose loop variable `x` ranges from `1` to `max+1`. The inner loop has a loop variable `y` that ranges from `1` to `x+1`, and the inner loop prints the value of `y`. The output of Listing 2.4 is here:

```
1
1 2
1 2 3
1 2 3 4
1 2 3 4 5
1 2 3 4 5 6
1 2 3 4 5 6 7
1 2 3 4 5 6 7 8
```

## THE `split()` FUNCTION WITH `for` LOOPS

`Python` supports various useful string-related functions, including the `split()` function and the `join()` function. The `split()` function is useful when you want to tokenize ("split") a line of text into words and then use a `for` loop to iterate through those words and process them accordingly.

The `join()` function does the opposite of `split()`: it "joins" two or more words into a single line. You can easily remove extra spaces in a sentence by using the `split()` function and then invoking the `join()` function, thereby creating a line of text with one white space between any two words.

## USING THE `split()` FUNCTION TO COMPARE WORDS

Listing 2.4 displays the contents of `Compare2.py` that illustrates how to use the split function to compare each word in a text string with another word.

***LISTING 2.4: Compare2.py***

```
x = 'This is a string that contains abc and Abc'
y = 'abc'
identical = 0
casematch = 0

for w in x.split():
  if(w == y):
    identical = identical + 1
  elif (w.lower() == y.lower()):
    casematch = casematch + 1

if(identical > 0):
 print('found identical matches:', identical)

if(casematch > 0):
 print('found case matches:', casematch)

if(casematch == 0 and identical == 0):
 print('no matches found')
```

Listing 2.4 uses the `split()` function in order to compare each word in the string x with the word `abc`. If there is an exact match, the variable `identical` is incremented. If a match does not occur, a case-insensitive match of the current word is performed with the string `abc`, and the variable `casematch` is incremented if the match is successful.

The output from Listing 2.5 is here:

```
found identical matches: 1
found case matches: 1
```

## USING THE `split()` FUNCTION TO PRINT JUSTIFIED TEXT

Listing 2.5 displays the contents of `FixedColumnCount.py` that illustrates how to print a set of words from a text string as justified text using a fixed number of columns.

***LISTING 2.5: FixedColumnCount1.py***

```
import string

wordCount = 0
str1 = 'this is a string with a set of words in it'

print('Left-justified strings:')
print('-----------------------')
```

```
for w in str1.split():
   print('%-10s' % w)
   wordCount = wordCount + 1
   if(wordCount % 2 == 0):
      print("")
print("\n")

print('Right-justified strings:')
print('-----------------------')

wordCount = 0
for w in str1.split():
   print('%10s' % w)
   wordCount = wordCount + 1
   if(wordCount % 2 == 0):
      print()
```

Listing 2.5 initializes the variables `wordCount` and `str1`, followed by two `for` loops. The first `for` loop prints the words in `str1` in left-justified format, and the second `for` loop prints the words in `str1` in right-justified format. In both loops, a linefeed is printed after a pair of consecutive words is printed, which occurs whenever the variable `wordCount` is even. The output from Listing 2.5 is here:

```
Left-justified strings:
-----------------------
this       is
a          string
with       a
set        of
words      in
it

Right-justified strings:
------------------------
      this        is
         a    string
      with         a
       set        of
     words        in
        it
```

## USING THE `split()` FUNCTION TO PRINT FIXED-WIDTH TEXT

Listing 2.6 displays the contents of `FixedColumnWidth1.py` that illustrates how to print a text string in a column of fixed width.

***LISTING 2.6: FixedColumnWidth1.py***

```
import string

left = 0
right = 0
columnWidth = 8
```

```
str1 = 'this is a string with a set of words in it and it
will be split into a fixed column width'
strLen = len(str1)

print('Left-justified column:')
print('----------------------')
rowCount = int(strLen/columnWidth)

for i in range(0,rowCount):
   left  = i*columnWidth
   right = (i+1)*columnWidth-1
   word  = str1[left:right]
   print("%-10s" % word)

# check for a 'partial row'
if(rowCount*columnWidth < strLen):
   left  = rowCount*columnWidth-1;
   right = strLen
   word  = str1[left:right]
   print("%-10s" % word)
```

Listing 2.6 initializes the integer variable `columnWidth` and the string variable `str1`. The variable `strLen` is the length of `str1`, and `rowCount` is `strLen` divided by `columnWidth`.

The next part of Listing 2.6 contains a loop that prints `rowCount` rows of characters, where each row contains `columnWidth` characters. The final portion of Listing 2.6 prints any "leftover" characters that comprise a partial row.

The newspaper-style output (but without any partial whitespace formatting) from Listing 2.6 is here:

```
Left-justified column:
----------------------
this is
a strin
 with a
set of
ords in
it and
t will
e split
into a
ixed co
umn wid
th
```

## USING THE `split()` FUNCTION TO COMPARE TEXT STRINGS

Listing 2.7 displays the contents of `CompareStrings1.py` that illustrates how to determine whether or not the words in one text string are also words in a second text string.

***LISTING 2.7: CompareStrings1.py***

```
text1 = 'a b c d'
text2 = 'a b c e d'

if(text2.find(text1) >= 0):
  print('text1 is a substring of text2')
else:
  print('text1 is not a substring of text2')

subStr = True
for w in text1.split():
  if(text2.find(w) == -1):
    subStr = False
    break

if(subStr == True):
  print('Every word in text1 is a word in text2')
else:
  print('Not every word in text1 is a word in text2')
```

Listing 2.7 initializes the string variables `text1` and `text2` and uses conditional logic to determine whether or not `text1` is a substring of `text2` (and then prints a suitable message).

The next part of Listing 2.7 is a loop that iterates through the words in the string `text1` and checks if each of those words is also a word in the string `text2`. If a nonmatch occurs, the variable `subStr` is set to False, followed by the break statement that causes an early exit from the loop. The final portion of Listing 2.7 prints the appropriate message based on the value of `subStr`. The output from Listing 2.7 is here:

```
text1 is not a substring of text2
Every word in text1 is a word in text2
```

## USING THE `split()` FUNCTION TO DISPLAY CHARACTERS IN A STRING

Listing 2.8 displays the contents of `StringChars1.py` that illustrates how to print the characters in a text string.

***LISTING 2.8: StringChars1.py***

```
text = 'abcdef'
for ch in text:
   print('char:',ch,'ord value:',ord(ch))
print
```

Listing 2.8 is straightforward: a `for` loop iterates through the characters in the string `text` and then prints the character and its `ord` value. The output from Listing 2.8 is here:

```
('char:', 'a', 'ord value:', 97)
('char:', 'b', 'ord value:', 98)
('char:', 'c', 'ord value:', 99)
('char:', 'd', 'ord value:', 100)
('char:', 'e', 'ord value:', 101)
('char:', 'f', 'ord value:', 102)
```

## THE `join()` FUNCTION

Another way to remove extraneous spaces is to use the `join()` function, as shown here:

```
text1 = '   there are      extra    spaces     '
print('text1:',text1)

text2 = ' '.join(text1.split())
print('text2:',text2)

text2 = 'XYZ'.join(text1.split())
print('text2:',text2)
```

The `split()` function "splits" a text string into a set of words, and also removes the extraneous white spaces. Next, the `join()` function "joins" together the words in the string `text1`, using a single white space as the delimiter. The last code portion of the preceding code block uses the string `XYZ` as the delimiter instead of a single white space.

The output of the preceding code block is here:

```
text1:    there are      extra    spaces
text2: there are extra spaces
text2: thereXYZareXYZextraXYZspaces
```

## PYTHON `while` LOOPS

You can define a `while` loop to iterate through a set of numbers, as shown in the following examples:

```
>>> x = 0
>>> while x < 5:
...    print(x)
...    x = x + 1
...
0
1
2
3
4
5
```

Python uses indentation instead of curly braces that are used in other languages such as JavaScript and Java. Although Python lists are not discussed until Chapter 3, you can probably understand the following simple code block that contains a variant of the preceding loop that you can use when working with lists:

```
lst  = [1,2,3,4]

while lst:
  print('list:',lst)
  print('item:',lst.pop())
```

The preceding while loop terminates when the lst variable is empty, and there is no need to explicitly test for an empty list. The output from the preceding code is here:

```
list: [1, 2, 3, 4]
item: 4
list: [1, 2, 3]
item: 3
list: [1, 2]
item: 2
list: [1]
item: 1
```

This concludes the examples that use the split() function in order to process words and characters in a text string. The next part of this chapter shows you examples of using conditional logic in Python code.

## CONDITIONAL LOGIC IN PYTHON

If you have written code in other programming languages, you have undoubtedly seen if/then/else (or if-elseif-else) conditional statements. Although the syntax varies between languages, the logic is essentially the same. The following example shows you how to use if/elif statements in Python:

```
>>> x = 25
>>> if x < 0:
...   print('negative')
... elif x < 25:
...   print('under 25')
... elif x == 25:
...   print('exactly 25')
... else:
...  print('over 25')
...
exactly 25
```

The preceding code block illustrates how to use multiple conditional statements, and the output is exactly what you expected.

## THE break/continue/pass STATEMENTS

The break statement in Python enables you to perform an "early exit" from a loop, whereas the continue statement essentially returns to the top of the loop and continues with the next value of the loop variable. The pass statement is essentially a "do nothing" statement.

Listing 2.9 displays the contents of BreakContinuePass.py that illustrates the use of these three statements.

***LISTING 2.9: BreakContinuePass.py***

```
print('first loop')
for x in range(1,4):
  if(x == 2):
    break
  print(x)

print('second loop')
for x in range(1,4):
  if(x == 2):
    continue
  print(x)

print('third loop')
for x in range(1,4):
  if(x == 2):
    pass
  print(x)
```

The output of Listing 2.9 is here:

```
first loop
1
second loop
1
3
third loop
1
2
3
```

## COMPARISON AND BOOLEAN OPERATORS

Python supports a variety of Boolean operators, such as in, not in, is, is not, and, or, and not. The next several sections discuss these operators and provide some examples of how to use them.

### The in/not in/is/is not Comparison Operators

The in and not in operators are used with sequences to check whether a value occurs or does not occur in a sequence. The operators is and is not determine whether or not two objects are the same object, which is important only matters for mutable objects such as lists. All comparison operators have the same priority, which is lower than that of all numerical operators. Comparisons can also be chained. For example, `a < b == c` tests whether `a` is less than `b` and moreover `b` equals `c`.

## The and, or, and not Boolean Operators

The Boolean operators `and`, `or`, and `not` have lower priority than comparison operators. The Boolean `and` and `or` are binary operators whereas the `Boolean or` operator is a unary operator. Here are some examples:

- `A and B` can only be true if both A and B are true
- `A or B` is true if either A or B is true
- `not(A)` is true if and only if A is false

You can also assign the result of a comparison or other `Boolean` expression to a variable, as shown here:

```
>>> string1, string2, string3 = '', 'b', 'cd'
>>> str4 = string1 or string2 or string3
>>> str4
'b'
```

The preceding code block initializes the variables `string1`, `string2`, and `string3`, where `string1` is an empty string. Next, `str4` is initialized via the `or` operator, and since the first nonnull value is `string2`, the value of `str4` is equal to `string2`.

# LOCAL AND GLOBAL VARIABLES

`Python` variables can be local or global. A `Python` variable is local to a function if the following are true:

- a parameter of the function
- on the left-side of a statement in the function
- bound to a control structure (such as for, with, and except)

A variable that is referenced in a function but is not local (according to the previous list) is a nonlocal variable. You can specify a variable as nonlocal with this snippet:

```
nonlocal z
```

A variable can be explicitly declared as global with this statement:

```
global z
```

The following code block illustrates the behavior of a global versus a local variable:

```
global z
z = 3

def changeVar(z):
  z = 4
  print('z in function:',z)

print('first global z:',z)

if __name__ == '__main__':
  changeVar(z)
  print('second global z:',z)
```

The output from the preceding code block is here:

```
first global z: 3
z in function: 4
second global z: 3
```

### Uninitialized Variables and the Value None

Python distinguishes between an uninitialized variable and the value None. The former is a variable that has not been assigned a value, whereas the value None is a value that indicates "no value" Collections and methods often return the value None, and you can test for the value None in conditional logic.

## SCOPE OF VARIABLES

The accessibility or scope of a variable depends on where that variable has been defined. Python provides two scopes: global and local, with the added "twist" that global is actually module-level scope (i.e., the current file), and therefore you can have a variable with the same name in different files and they will be treated differently.

Local variables are straightforward: they are defined inside a function, and they can only be accessed inside the function where they are defined. Any variables that are not local variables have global scope, which means that those variables are "global" *only* with respect to the file where it has been defined, and they can be accessed anywhere in a file.

There are two scenarios to consider regarding variables. First, suppose two files (aka modules) file1.py and file2.py have a variable called x, and file1.py also imports file2.py. The question now is how to disambiguate between the x in the two different modules. As an example, suppose that file2.py contains the following two lines of code:

```
x = 3
print('unscoped x in file2:',x)
```

Suppose that `file1.py` contains the following code:

```
import file2 as file2

x = 5
print('unscoped x in file1:',x)
print('scoped x from file2:',file2.x)
```

Launch `file1.y` from the command line, and you will see the following output:

```
unscoped x in file2: 3
unscoped x in file1: 5
scoped x from file2: 3
```

The second scenario involves a program that contains a local variable and a global variable with the same name. According to the earlier rule, the local variable is used in the function where it is defined, and the global variable is used outside of that function.

The following code block illustrates the use of a global and local variable with the same name:

```
#!/usr/bin/python
# a global variable:
total = 0;

def sum(x1, x2):
   # this total is local:
   total = x1+x2;

   print("Local total : ", total)
   return total

# invoke the sum function
sum(2,3);
print("Global total : ", total)
```

When the above code is executed, it produces following result:

```
Local total :   5
Global total :  0
```

What about unscoped variables, such as specifying the variable `x` without a module prefix? The answer consists of the following sequence of steps that `Python` will perform:

1. Check the local scope for the name.
2. Ascend the enclosing scopes and check for the name.
3. Perform Step 2 until the global scope is found (i.e., module level)
4. If x still hasn't been found, Python checks__builtins__.

As an illustration, type python at the command line and then enter the statements that are preceded with three angle brackets (">>>"):

```
Python 3.9.1 (v3.9.1:1e5d33e9b9, Dec  7 2020, 12:44:01)
[Clang 12.0.0 (clang-1200.0.32.27)] on darwin
Type "help", "copyright", "credits" or "license" for more
information.
>>> x = 1
>>> g = globals()
>>> g
{'__name__': '__main__', '__doc__': None, '__package__':
None, '__loader__': <class '_frozen_importlib.
BuiltinImporter'>, '__spec__': None, '__annotations__': {},
'__builtins__': <module 'builtins' (built-in)>, 'x': 1,
'g': {...}}
>>> g.pop('x')
1
>>> x
Traceback (most recent call last):
  File "<stdin>", line 1, in <module>
NameError: name 'x' is not defined
```

**NOTE** *You can access the* `dicts` *that Python uses to track local and global scope by invoking* `locals()` *and* `globals()` *respectively.*

## PASS BY REFERENCE VERSUS VALUE

All parameters (arguments) in the `Python` language are passed by reference. Thus, if you change what a parameter refers to within a function, the change is reflected in the calling function. For example:

```
def changeme(mylist):
   #This changes a passed list into this function
   mylist.append([1,2,3,4])
   print("Values inside the function: ", mylist)
   return

# Now you can call changeme function
mylist = [10,20,30]
changeme(mylist)
print("Values outside the function: ", mylist)
```

Here we are maintaining reference of the passed object and appending values in the same object, and the result is shown here:

```
Values inside the function:  [10, 20, 30, [1, 2, 3, 4]]
Values outside the function:  [10, 20, 30, [1, 2, 3, 4]]
```

The fact that values are passed by reference gives rise to the notion of mutability versus immutability that is discussed in Chapter 3.

## ARGUMENTS AND PARAMETERS

`Python` differentiates between arguments to functions and parameter declarations in functions: a positional (mandatory) and keyword (optional/default value). This concept is important because Python has operators for packing and unpacking these kinds of arguments.

Python unpacks positional arguments from an iterable, as shown here:

```
>>> def foo(x, y):
...   return x - y
...
>>> data = 4,5
>>> foo(data) # only passed one arg
Traceback (most recent call last):
  File "<stdin>", line 1, in <module>
TypeError: foo() takes exactly 2 arguments (1 given)
>>> foo(*data) # passed however many args are in tuple
-1
```

## USING A while LOOP TO FIND THE DIVISORS OF A NUMBER

Listing 2.10 contains a `while` loop, conditional logic, and the `%` (modulus) operator in order to find the factors of any integer greater than `1`.

***LISTING 2.10: Divisors.py***

```
def divisors(num):
  div = 2

  while(num > 1):
    if(num % div == 0):
      print("divisor: ", div)
      num = num / div
    else:
      div = div + 1
  print("** finished **")

divisors(12)
```

Listing 2.10 defines a function `divisors()` that takes an integer value `num` and then initializes the variable `div` with the value `2`. The `while` loop divides `num` by `div` and if the remainder is `0`, it prints the value of `div` and then it divides `num` by `div`; if the value is not `0`, then `div` is incremented by 1. This `while` loop continues as long as the value of `num` is greater than `1`.

The output from Listing 2.10 passing in the value `12` to the function `divisors()` is here:

```
divisor:  2
divisor:  2
divisor:  3
** finished **
```

Listing 2.11 displays the contents of `Divisors2.py` that contains a `while` loop, conditional logic, and the % (modulus) operator in order to find the factors of any integer greater than `1`.

*LISTING 2.11: Divisors2.py*

```
def divisors(num):
  primes = ""
  div = 2

  while(num > 1):
    if(num % div == 0):
      divList = divList + str(div) + ' '
      num = num / div
    else:
      div = div + 1
  return divList

result = divisors(12)
print('The divisors of',12,'are:',result)
```

Listing 2.11 is very similar to Listing 2.10: the main difference is that Listing 2.10 constructs the variable `divList` (which is a concatenated list of the divisors of a number) in the `while` loop, and then returns the value of `divList` when the `while` loop has completed. The output from Listing 2.11 is here:

```
The divisors of 12 are: 2 2 3
```

## Using a `while` loop to Find Prime Numbers

Listing 2.12 displays the contents of `Divisors3.py` that contains a `while` loop, conditional logic, and the % (modulus) operator in order to count the number of prime factors of any integer greater than 1. If there is only one divisor for a number, then that number is a prime number.

*LISTING 2.12: Divisors3.py*

```
def divisors(num):
  count = 1
  div = 2
  while(div < num):
    if(num % div == 0):
      count = count + 1
    div = div + 1
  return count

result = divisors(12)

if(result == 1):
  print('12 is prime')
else:
  print('12 is not prime')
```

## USER-DEFINED FUNCTIONS IN PYTHON

`Python` provides built-in functions and also enables you to define your own functions. You can define functions to provide the required functionality. Here are simple rules to define a function in Python:

- Function blocks begin with the keyword `def` followed by the function name and parentheses.
- Any input arguments should be placed within these parentheses.
- The first statement of a function can be an optional statement—the documentation string of the function or docstring.
- The code block within every function starts with a colon (:) and is indented.
- The statement return [expression] exits a function, optionally passing back an expression to the caller. A return statement with no arguments is the same as return "None."
- If a function does not specify a return statement, the function automatically returns "None," which is a special type of value in Python.

A very simple custom Python function is here:

```
>>> def func():
...   print 3
...
>>> func()
3
```

The preceding function is trivial, but it does illustrate the syntax for defining custom functions in Python. The following example is slightly more useful:

```
>>> def func(x):
...   for i in range(0,x):
...     print(i)
...
>>> func(5)
0
1
2
3
4
```

## SPECIFYING DEFAULT VALUES IN A FUNCTION

Listing 2.13 displays the contents of `DefaultValues.py` that illustrates how to specify default values in a function.

***LISTING 2.13: DefaultValues.py***

```
def numberFunc(a, b=10):
  print (a,b)

def stringFunc(a, b='xyz'):
  print (a,b)

def collectionFunc(a, b=None):
  if(b is None):
     print('No value assigned to b')

numberFunc(3)
stringFunc('one')
collectionFunc([1,2,3])
```

Listing 2.13 defines three functions, followed by an invocation of each of those functions. The functions `numberFunc()` and `stringFunc()` print a list containing the values of their two parameters, and `collectionFunc()` displays a message if the second parameter is `None`. The output from Listing 2.13 is here:

```
(3, 10)
('one', 'xyz')
No value assigned to b
```

## Returning Multiple Values From a Function

This task is accomplished by the code in Listing 2.14, which displays the contents of `MultipleValues.py`.

***LISTING 2.14: MultipleValues.py***

```
def MultipleValues():
    return 'a', 'b', 'c'

x, y, z = MultipleValues()

print('x:',x)
print('y:',y)
print('z:',z)
```

The output from Listing 2.14 is here:

```
x: a
y: b
z: c
```

# FUNCTIONS WITH A VARIABLE NUMBER OF ARGUMENTS

`Python` enables you to define functions with a variable number of arguments. This functionality is useful in many situations, such as computing the sum, average, or product of a set of numbers. For example, the following code block computes the sum of two numbers:

```
def sum(a, b):
    return a + b
```

```
values = (1, 2)
s1 = sum(*values)
print('s1 = ', s1)
```

The output of the preceding code block is here:

```
s1 =  3
```

However, the `sum` function in the preceding code block can only be used for two numeric values.

Listing 2.15 displays the contents of `VariableSum1.py` that illustrates how to compute the sum of a variable number of numbers.

***LISTING 2.15: VariableSum1.py***

```
def sum(*values):
  sum = 0
  for x in values:
    sum = sum + x
  return sum

values1 = (1, 2)
s1 = sum(*values1)
print('s1 = ',s1)

values2 = (1, 2, 3, 4)
s2 = sum(*values2)
print('s2 = ',s2)
```

Listing 2.15 defines the function sum whose parameter values can be an arbitrary list of numbers. The next portion of this function initializes sum to `0`, and then a `for` loop iterates through values and adds each of its elements to the variable `sum`. The last line in the function `sum()` returns the value of the variable `sum`. The output from Listing 2.15 is here:

```
s1 =  3
s2 =  10
```

## LAMBDA EXPRESSIONS

Listing 2.16 displays the contents of `Lambda1.py` that illustrates how to create a simple lambda function in `Python`.

***LISTING 2.16 Lambda1.py***

```
add = lambda x, y: x + y

x1 = add(5,7)
x2 = add('Hello', 'Python')

print(x1)
print(x2)
```

Listing 2.16 defines the lambda expression add that accepts two input parameters and then returns their sum (for numbers) or their concatenation (for strings).

The output from Listing 2.16 is here:

```
12
HelloPython
```

## RECURSION

Recursion is a powerful technique that can provide an elegant solution to various problems. The following subsections contain examples of using recursion to calculate some well-known numbers.

### Calculating Factorial Values

The factorial value of a positive integer `n` is the product of all the integers between `1` and `n`. The symbol for factorial is the exclamation point ("!") and some sample factorial values are here:

```
1! = 1
2! = 2
3! = 6
4! = 20
5! = 120
```

The formula for the factorial value of a number is succinctly defined as follows:

```
Factorial(n) = n*Factorial(n-1) for n > 1 and Factorial(1) = 1
```

Listing 2.17 displays the contents of `Factorial.py` that illustrates how to use recursion in order to calculate the factorial value of a positive integer.

***LISTING 2.17: Factorial.py***

```
def factorial(num):

  if (num > 1):
    return num * factorial(num-1)
  else:
    return 1

result = factorial(5)
print('The factorial of 5 =', result)
```

Listing 2.17 contains the function `factorial` that implements the recursive definition of the factorial value of a number. The output from Listing 2.17 is here:

```
The factorial of 5 = 120
```

In addition to a recursive solution, there is also an iterative solution for calculating the factorial value of a number. Listing 2.18 displays the contents of `Factorial2.py` that illustrates how to use the `range()` function in order to calculate the factorial value of a positive integer.

***LISTING 2.18: Factorial2.py***

```
def factorial2(num):
  prod = 1
  for x in range(1,num+1):
    prod = prod * x
  return prod

result = factorial2(5)
print 'The factorial of 5 =', result
```

Listing 2.18 defines the function `factorial2()` with a parameter `num`, followed by the variable `prod` which has an initial value of 1. The next part of `factorial2()` is a `for` loop whose loop variable `x` ranges between `1` and `num+1`, and each iteration through that loop multiples the value of `prod` with the value of `x`, thereby computing the factorial value of `num`. The output from Listing 2.18 is here:

```
The factorial of 5 = 120
```

## Calculating Fibonacci Numbers

The set of Fibonacci numbers represent some interesting patterns (such as the pattern of a sunflower) in nature, and its recursive definition is here:

```
Fib(0) = 0
Fib(1) = 1
Fib(n) = Fib(n-1) + Fib(n-2) for n >= 2
```

Listing 2.19 displays the contents of `fib.py` that illustrates how to calculate Fibonacci numbers.

***LISTING 2.19: fib.py***

```
def fib(num):
  if (num == 0):
    return 1
  elif (num == 1):
    return 1
  else:
    return fib(num-1) + fib(num-2)

result = fib(10)
print('Fibonacci value of 5 =', result)
```

Listing 2.19 defines the fib() function with the parameter num. If num equals 0 or 1 then fib() returns num; otherwise, fib() returns the result of adding fib(num-1) and fib(num-2). The output from Listing 2.19 is here:

```
Fibonacci value of 10 = 89
```

## Calculating the GCD of Two Numbers

The GCD (greatest common divisor) of two positive integers is the largest integer that divides both integers with a remainder of 0. Some values are shown here:

```
gcd(6,2)   = 2
gcd(10,4)  = 2
gcd(24,16) = 8
```

Listing 2.20 uses recursion and Euclid's algorithm in order to find the GCD of two positive integers.

***LISTING: 2.20 gcd.py***

```
def gcd(num1, num2):
  if(num1 % num2 == 0):
    return num2
  elif (num1 < num2):
    print("switching ", num1, " and ", num2)
    return gcd(num2, num1)
  else:
    print("reducing", num1, " and ", num2)
    return gcd(num1-num2, num2)

result = gcd(24, 10)
print("GCD of", 24, "and", 10, "=", result)
```

Listing 2.20 defines the function gcd() with the parameters num1 and num2. If num1 is divisible by num2, the function returns num2. If num1 is less than num2, then gcd is invoked by switching the order of num1 and num2. In all other cases, gcd() returns the result of computing gcd() with the values num1-num2 and num2. The output from Listing 2.20 is here:

```
reducing 24  and  10
reducing 14  and  10
switching  4  and  10
reducing 10  and  4
reducing 6  and  4
switching  2  and  4
GCD of 24 and 10 = 2
```

## Calculating the LCM of Two Numbers

The LCM (lowest common multiple) of two positive integers is the smallest integer that is a multiple of those two integers. Some values are shown here:

```
lcm(6,2)    = 2
lcm(10,4)   = 20
lcm(24,16)  = 48
```

In general, if x and y are two positive integers, you can calculate their LCM as follows:

```
lcm(x,y) = x/gcd(x,y)*y/gcd(x,y)
```

Listing 2.21 uses the `gcd()` function that is defined in the previous section in order to calculate the LCM of two positive integers.

***LISTING 2.21: lcm.py***

```
def gcd(num1, num2):
  if(num1 % num2 == 0):
    return num2
  elif (num1 < num2):
   #print("switching ", num1, " and ", num2)
    return gcd(num2, num1)
  else:
   #print("reducing", num1, " and ", num2)
    return gcd(num1-num2, num2)

def lcm(num1, num2):
  gcd1 = gcd(num1, num2)
  lcm1 = num1*num2/gcd1
  return lcm1

result = lcm(24, 10)
print("The LCM of", 24, "and", 10, "=", result)
```

Listing 2.21 defines the function `gcd()` that was discussed in the previous section, followed by the function lcm that takes the parameters `num1` and `num2`. The first line in `lcm()` computes gcd1, which is the `gcd()` of `num1` and `num2`. The second line in `lcm()` computes `lcm1`, which is `num1` divided by three values. The third line in `lcm()` returns the value of `lcm1`. The output of Listing 2.21 is here:

```
The LCM of 24 and 10 = 60
```

## SUMMARY

This chapter showed you how to use conditional logic in Python. You also learned how to work with loops in `Python`, including `for` loops and `while` loops. You learned how to compute various values, such as the GCD (greatest common divisor) and LCM (lowest common multiple) of a pair of numbers, and also how to determine whether or not a positive integer is prime.

CHAPTER 3

# PYTHON DATA STRUCTURES

In Chapters 1 and 2, you learned how to work with numbers and strings, as well as control structures in `Python`. This chapter discusses `Python` collections, such as lists (or arrays), sets, tuples, and dictionaries. You will see many short code blocks that will help you rapidly learn how to work with these data structures in `Python`. After you have finished reading this chapter, you will be in a better position to create more complex Python modules using one or more of these data structures.

The first part of this chapter discusses `Python` lists and shows you code samples that illustrate various methods that are available for manipulating lists. The second part of this chapter discusses Python sets and how they differ from `Python` lists. The third part of this chapter discusses `Python` tuples, and the final part of this chapter discusses Python dictionaries.

## WORKING WITH LISTS

Python supports a list data type, along with a rich set of list-related functions. Since lists are not typed, you can create a list of different data types, as well as multidimensional lists. The next several sections show you how to manipulate list structures in Python.

### Lists and Basic Operations

A `Python` list consists of comma-separated values enclosed in a pair of square brackets. The following examples illustrate the syntax for defining a list in Python, and also how to perform various operations on a `Python` list:

```
>>> list = [1, 2, 3, 4, 5]
>>> list
[1, 2, 3, 4, 5]
>>> list[2]
3
```

```
>>> list2 = list + [1, 2, 3, 4, 5]
>>> list2
[1, 2, 3, 4, 5, 1, 2, 3, 4, 5]
>>> list2.append(6)
>>> list2
[1, 2, 3, 4, 5, 1, 2, 3, 4, 5, 6]
>>> len(list)
5
>>> x = ['a', 'b', 'c']
>>> y = [1, 2, 3]
>>> z = [x, y]
>>> z[0]
['a', 'b', 'c']
>>> len(x)
3
```

You can assign multiple variables to a list, provided that the number and type of the variables match the structure. Here is an example:

```
>>> point = [7,8]
>>> x,y = point
>>> x
7
>>> y
8
```

The following example shows you how to assign values to variables from a more complex data structure:

```
>>> line = ['a', 10, 20, (2024,01,31)]
>>> x1,x2,x3,date1 = line
>>> x1
'a'
>>> x2
10
>>> x3
20
>>> date1
(2024, 1, 31
```

If you want to access the year/month/date components of the `date1` element in the preceding code block, you can do so with the following code block:

```
>>> line = ['a', 10, 20, (2024,01,31)]
>>> x1,x2,x3,(year,month,day) = line
>>> x1
'a'
>>> x2
10
>>> x3
20
>>> year
2024
>>> month
```

```
1
>>> day
31
```

If the number and/or structure of the variables do not match the data, an error message is displayed, as shown here:

```
>>> point = (1,2)
>>> x,y,z = point
Traceback (most recent call last):
  File "<stdin>", line 1, in <module>
ValueError: need more than 2 values to unpack
```

If the number of variables that you specify is less than the number of data items, you will see an error message, as shown here:

```
>>> line = ['a', 10, 20, (2014,01,31)]
>>> x1,x2 = line
Traceback (most recent call last):
  File "<stdin>", line 1, in <module>
ValueError: too many values to unpack
```

## Reversing and Sorting a List

The Python `reverse()` method reverses the contents of a list, as shown here:

```
>>> a = [4, 1, 2, 3]
>>> a.reverse()
[3, 2, 1, 4]
```

The Python `sort()` method sorts a list:

```
>>> a = [4, 1, 2, 3]
>>> a.sort()
[1, 2, 3, 4]
```

You can sort a list and then reverse its contents, as shown here:

```
>>> a = [4, 1, 2, 3]
>>> a.reverse(a.sort())
[4, 3, 2, 1]
```

Another way to reverse a list:

```
>>> L = [0,10,20,40]
>>> L[::-1]
[40, 20, 10, 0]
```

Keep in mind is that `reversed(array)` is an iterable and not a list. However, you can convert the reversed array to a list with this code snippet:

```
list(reversed(array)) or L[::-1]
```

Listing 3.1 contains a `while` loop whose logic is the opposite of the listing in the previous section: if `num` is divisible by multiple numbers (each of which is strictly less than `num`), then `num` is not prime.

***LISTING 3.1: Uppercase1.py***

```
list1 = ['a', 'list', 'of', 'words']
list2 = [s.upper() for s in list1]
list3 = [s for s in list1 if len(s) <=2 ]
list4 = [s for s in list1 if 'w' in s ]

print('list1:',list1)
print('list2:',list2)
print('list3:',list3)
print('list4:',list4)
```

The output from launching the code in Listing 3.1 is here:

```
list1: ['a', 'list', 'of', 'words']
list2: ['A', 'LIST', 'OF', 'WORDS']
list3: ['a', 'of']
list4: ['words']
```

## Lists and Arithmetic Operations

The minimum value of a list of numbers is the first number of in the sorted list of numbers. If you reverse the sorted list, the first number is the maximum value. There are several ways to reverse a list, starting with the technique shown in the following code:

```
x = [3,1,2,4]
maxList = x.sort()
minList = x.sort(x.reverse())

min1 = min(x)
max1 = max(x)
print min1
print max1
```

The output of the preceding code block is here:

```
1
4
```

A second (and better) way to sort a list is shown here:

```
minList = x.sort(reverse=True)
```

A third way to sort a list involves the built-in functional version of the `sort()` method, as shown here:

```
sorted(x, reverse=True)
```

The preceding code snippet is useful when you do not want to modify the original order of the list or you want to compose multiple list operations on a single line.

## Lists and Filter-Related Operations

Python enables you to filter a list (also called list comprehension) as shown here:

```
mylist = [1, -2, 3, -5, 6, -7, 8]
pos = [n for n in mylist if n > 0]
neg = [n for n in mylist if n < 0]

print pos
print neg
```

You can also specify `if/else` logic in a filter, as shown here:

```
mylist = [1, -2, 3, -5, 6, -7, 8]
negativeList = [n if n < 0 else 0 for n in mylist]
positiveList = [n if n > 0 else 0 for n in mylist]

print positiveList
print negativeList
```

The output of the preceding code block is here:

```
[1, 3, 6, 8]
[-2, -5, -7]
[1, 0, 3, 0, 6, 0, 8]
[0, -2, 0, -5, 0, -7, 0]
```

# SORTING LISTS OF NUMBERS AND STRINGS

Listing 3.2 displays the contents of the `Python` script `Sorted1.py` that determines whether or not two lists are sorted.

***LISTING 3.2: Sorted1.py***

```
list1 = [1,2,3,4,5]
list2 = [2,1,3,4,5]

sort1 = sorted(list1)
sort2 = sorted(list2)

if(list1 == sort1):
  print(list1,'is sorted')
else:
  print(list1,'is not sorted')

if(list2 == sort2):
  print(list2,'is sorted')
else:
  print(list2,'is not sorted')
```

Listing 3.2 initializes the lists `list1` and `list2`, and the sorted lists `sort1` and `sort2` based on the lists `list1` and `list2`, respectively. If `list1` equals `sort1` then `list1` is already sorted; similarly, if `list2` equals `sort2` then `list2` is already sorted.

The output from Listing 3.2 is here:

```
[1, 2, 3, 4, 5] is sorted
[2, 1, 3, 4, 5] is not sorted
```

Note that if you sort a list of character strings the output is case sensitive, and that uppercase letters appear before lowercase letters. This is due to the fact that the collating sequence for ASCII places uppercase letter (decimal `65` through decimal `91`) before lowercase letters (decimal `97` through decimal `127`). The following example provides an illustration:

```
>>> list1 = ['a', 'A', 'b', 'B', 'Z']
>>> print sorted(list1)
['A', 'B', 'Z', 'a', 'b']
```

You can also specify the reverse option so that the list is sorted in reverse order:

```
>>> list1 = ['a', 'A', 'b', 'B', 'Z']
>>> print sorted(list1, reverse=True)
['b', 'a', 'Z', 'B', 'A']
```

You can even sort a list based on the length of the items in the list:

```
>>> list1 = ['a', 'AA', 'bbb', 'BBBBB', 'ZZZZZZZ']
>>> print sorted(list1, key=len)
['a', 'AA', 'bbb', 'BBBBB', 'ZZZZZZZ']
>>> print sorted(list1, key=len, reverse=True)
['ZZZZZZZ', 'BBBBB', 'bbb', 'AA', 'a']
```

You can specify `str.lower` if you want treat uppercase letters as though they are lowercase letters during the sorting operation, as shown here:

```
>>> print sorted(list1, key=str.lower)
['a', 'AA', 'bbb', 'BBBBB', 'ZZZZZZZ']
```

## EXPRESSIONS IN LISTS

The following construct is similar to a `for` loop but without the colon ":" character that appears at the end of a loop construct. Consider the following example:

```
nums = [1, 2, 3, 4]
cubes = [n*n*n for n in nums]

print 'nums: ',nums
print 'cubes:',cubes
```

The output from the preceding code block is here:

```
nums:  [1, 2, 3, 4]
cubes: [1, 8, 27, 64]
```

## CONCATENATING A LIST OF WORDS

`Python` provides the `join()` method for concatenating text strings, as shown here:

```
>>> parts = ['Is', 'SF', 'In', 'California?']
>>> ' '.join(parts)
'Is SF In California?'
>>> ','.join(parts)
'Is,SF,In,California?'
>>> ''.join(parts) 'IsSFInCalifornia?'
```

There are several ways to concatenate a set of strings and then print the result. The following is the most inefficient way to do so:

```
print "This" + " is" + " a" + " sentence"
```

Either of the following is preferred:

```
print "%s %s %s %s" % ("This", "is", "a", "sentence")
print " ".join(["This","is","a","sentence"])
```

## THE BUBBLESORT IN PYTHON

The previous sections contain examples that illustrate how to sort a list of numbers using the `sort()` function. However, sometimes you need to implement different types of sorts in Python. Listing 3.3 displays the contents of `BubbleSort.py` that illustrates how to implement the Bubblesort in `Python`.

***LISTING 3.3: BubbleSort.py***

```
list1 = [1, 5, 3, 4]

print("Initial list:",list1)

for i in range(0,len(list1)-1):
  for j in range(i+1,len(list1)):
    if(list1[i] > list1[j]):
      temp = list1[i]
      list1[i] = list1[j]
      list1[j] = temp

print("Sorted list: ",list1)
```

The output from Listing 3.3 is here:

```
Initial list: [1, 5, 3, 4]
Sorted list:  [1, 3, 4, 5]
```

## THE PYTHON range() FUNCTION

In this section you will learn about the `Python range()` function that you can use to iterate through a list, as shown here:

```
>>> for i in range(0,5):
...    print i
...
0
1
2
3
4
```

You can use a `for` loop to iterate through a list of strings, as shown here:

```
>>> x
['a', 'b', 'c']
>>> for w in x:
...    print w
...
a
b
c
```

You can use a `for` loop to iterate through a list of strings and provide additional details, as shown here:

```
>>> x
['a', 'b', 'c']
>>> for w in x:
...    print len(w), w
...
1 a
1 b
1 c
```

The preceding output displays the length of each word in the list `x`, followed by the word itself.

### Counting Digits, Uppercase, and Lowercase Letters

Listing 3.4 displays the contents of the `Python` file `CountCharTypes.py` that counts the occurrences of digits and letters in a string.

***LISTING 3.4: Counter1.py***

```
str1 = "abc4234AFde"
digitCount = 0
alphaCount = 0
upperCount = 0
lowerCount = 0
```

```
for i in range(0,len(str1)):
  char = str1[i]
  if(char.isdigit()):
   #print("this is a digit:",char)
    digitCount += 1
  elif(char.isalpha()):
   #print("this is alphabetic:",char)
    alphaCount  += 1
    if(char.upper() == char):
      upperCount  += 1
    else:
      lowerCount  += 1

print('Original String:    ',str1)
print('Number of digits:   ',digitCount)
print('Total alphanumeric:',alphaCount)
print('Upper Case Count:   ',upperCount)
print('Lower Case Count:   ',lowerCount)
```

Listing 3.4 initializes counter-related variables, followed by a loop (with loop variable `i`) that iterates from `0` to the length of the string `str1`. The string variable `char` is initialized with the letter at index `i` of the string `str1`. The next portion of the loop uses conditional logic to determine whether `char` is a digit or an alphabetic character; in the latter case, the code checks whether or not the character is uppercase or lowercase. In all cases, the values of the appropriate counter-related variables are incremented.

The output of Listing 3.4 is here:

```
Original String:    abc4234AFde
Number of digits:   4
Total alphanumeric: 7
Upper Case Count:   2
Lower Case Count:   5
```

## ARRAYS AND THE `append()` FUNCTION

Although `Python` does have an array type (`import array`), which is essentially a heterogeneous list, the array type has no advantages over the list type other than a slight saving in memory use. You can also define heterogeneous arrays:

```
a = [10, 'hello', [5, '77']]
```

You can append a new element to an element inside a list:

```
>>> a = [10, 'hello', [5, '77']]
>>> a[2].append('abc')
>>> a
[10, 'hello', [5, '77', 'abc']]
```

You can assign simple variables to the elements of a list, as shown here:

```
myList = [ 'a', 'b', 91.1, (2014, 01, 31) ]
x1, x2, x3, x4 = myList
print 'x1:',x1
print 'x2:',x2
print 'x3:',x3
print 'x4:',x4
```

The output of the preceding code block is here:

```
x1: a
x2: b
x3: 91.1
x4: (2014, 1, 31)
```

The Python `split()` function is more convenient (especially when the number of elements is unknown or variable) than the preceding sample, and you will see examples of the `split()` function in the next section.

## WORKING WITH LISTS AND THE split() FUNCTION

You can use the `Python split()` function to split the words in a text string and populate a list with those words. An example is here:

```
>>> x = "this is a string"
>>> list = x.split()
>>> list
['this', 'is', 'a', 'string']
```

A simple way to print the list of words in a text string is shown here:

```
>>> x = "this is a string"
>>> for w in x.split():
...   print w
...
this
is
a
string
```

You can search for a word in a string as follows:

```
>>> x = "this is a string"
>>> for w in x.split():
...    if(w == 'this'):
...      print "x contains this"
...
x contains this
...
```

## COUNTING WORDS IN A LIST

`Python` provides the `Counter` class that enables you to count the words in a list. Listing 3.5 displays the contents of `CountWord2.py` that displays the top three words with greatest frequency.

***LISTING 3.5: CountWord2.py***

```
from collections import Counter

mywords = ['a', 'b', 'a', 'b', 'c', 'a', 'd', 'e', 'f', 'b']

word_counts = Counter(mywords)
topThree = word_counts.most_common(3)
print(topThree)
```

Listing 3.5 initializes the variable `mywords` with a set of characters and then initializes the variable `word_counts` by passing `mywords` as an argument to `Counter`. The variable `topThree` is an array containing the three most common characters (and their frequency) that appear in `mywords`. The output from Listing 3.5 is here:

```
[('a', 3), ('b', 3), ('c', 1)]
```

## ITERATING THROUGH PAIRS OF LISTS

`Python` supports operations on pairs of lists, which means that you can perform vector-like operations. The following snippet multiplies every list element by 3:

```
>>> list1 = [1, 2, 3]
>>> [3*x for x in list1]
[3, 6, 9]
```

Create a new list with pairs of elements consisting of the original element and the original element multiplied by 3:

```
>>> list1 = [1, 2, 3]
>>> [[x, 3*x] for x in list1]
[[1, 3], [2, 6], [3, 9]]
```

Compute the product of every pair of numbers from two lists:

```
>>> list1 = [1, 2, 3]
>>> list2 = [5, 6, 7]
>>> [a*b for a in list1 for b in list2]
[5, 6, 7, 10, 12, 14, 15, 18, 21]
```

Calculate the sum of every pair of numbers from two lists:

```
>>> list1 = [1, 2, 3]
>>> list2 = [5, 6, 7]
>>> [a+b for a in list1 for b in list2]
[6, 7, 8, 7, 8, 9, 8, 9, 10]
```

Calculate the pair-wise product of two lists:

```
>>> [list1[i]*list2[i] for i in range(len(list1))]
[8, 12, -54]
```

## OTHER LIST-RELATED FUNCTIONS

`Python` provides additional functions that you can use with lists, such as `append()`, `insert()`, `delete()`, `pop()`, and `extend()`. `Python` also supports the functions `index()`, `count()`, `sort()`, and `reverse()`. Examples of these functions are illustrated in the following code block.

Define a Python list (notice that duplicates are allowed):

```
>>> a = [1, 2, 3, 2, 4, 2, 5]
```

Display the number of occurrences of 1 and 2:

```
>>> print a.count(1), a.count(2)
1 3
```

Insert -8 in position 3:

```
>>> a.insert(3,-8)
>>> a
[1, 2, 3, -8, 2, 4, 2, 5]
```

Remove occurrences of 3:

```
>>> a.remove(3)
>>> a
[1, 2, -8, 2, 4, 2, 5]
```

Remove occurrences of 1:

```
>>> a.remove(1)
>>> a
[2, -8, 2, 4, 2, 5]
```

Append 19 to the list:

```
>>> a.append(19)
>>> a
[2, -8, 2, 4, 2, 5, 19]
```

Print the index of 19 in the list:

```
>>> a.index(19)
6
```

Reverse the list:

```
>>> a.reverse()
>>> a
[19, 5, 2, 4, 2, -8, 2]
```

Sort the list:

```
>>> a.sort()
>>> a
[-8, 2, 2, 2, 4, 5, 19]
```

Extend list a with list b:

```
>>> b = [100,200,300]
>>> a.extend(b)
>>> a
[-8, 2, 2, 2, 4, 5, 19, 100, 200, 300]
```

Remove the first occurrence of 2:

```
>>> a.pop(2)
2
>>> a
[-8, 2, 2, 4, 5, 19, 100, 200, 300]
```

Remove the last item of the list:

```
>>> a.pop()
300
>>> a
[-8, 2, 2, 4, 5, 19, 100, 200]
```

Now that you understand how to use list-related operations, the next section shows you how to use a Python list as a stack.

## USING A LIST AS A STACK AND A QUEUE

A stack is a LIFO ("Last In First Out") data structure with `push()` and `pop()` functions for adding and removing elements, respectively. The most recently added element in a stack is in the top position, and therefore the first element that can be removed from the stack.

The following code block illustrates how to create a stack and also remove and append items from a stack in `Python`. Create a `Python` list (which we'll use as a stack):

```
>>> s = [1,2,3,4]
```

Append 5 to the stack:

```
>>> s.append(5)
>>> s
[1, 2, 3, 4, 5]
```

Remove the last element from the stack:

```
>>> s.pop()
5
>>> s
[1, 2, 3, 4]
```

A queue is a FIFO (First In First Out) data structure with `insert()` and `pop()` functions for inserting and removing elements, respectively. The most recently added element in a queue is in the top position, and therefore is the last element that can be removed from the queue.

The following code block illustrates how to create a queue and also insert and append items to a queue in Python.

Create a `Python` list (which we'll use as a queue):

```
>>> q = [1,2,3,4]
```

Insert 5 at the beginning of the queue:

```
>>> q.insert(0,5)
>>> q
[5, 1, 2, 3, 4]
```

Remove the last element from the queue:

```
>>> q.pop(0)
1
>>> q
[5, 2, 3, 4]
```

The preceding code uses `q.insert(0, 5)` to insert in the beginning and `q.pop()` to remove from the end. However, keep in mind that the `insert()` operation is slow in `Python`: insert at `0` requires copying all the elements in underlying array down one space. Therefore, use `collections.deque` with `coll.appendleft()` and `coll.pop()`, where `coll` is an instance of the `Collection` class.

The next section shows you how to work with vectors in Python.

## WORKING WITH VECTORS

A vector is a one-dimensional array of values, and you can perform vector-based operations, such as addition, subtraction, and inner product. Listing 3.6 displays the contents of `MyVectors.py` that illustrates how to perform vector-based operations.

***LISTING 3.6: MyVectors.py***

```
v1 = [1,2,3]
v2 = [1,2,3]
v3 = [5,5,5]

s1 = [0,0,0]
d1 = [0,0,0]
p1 = 0

print("Initial Vectors")
print('v1:',v1)
print('v2:',v2)
print('v3:',v3)

for i in range(len(v1)):
    d1[i] = v3[i] - v2[i]
    s1[i] = v3[i] + v2[i]
    p1    = v3[i] * v2[i] + p1

print("After operations")
print('d1:',d1)
print('s1:',s1)
print('p1:',p1)
```

Listing 3.6 starts with the definition of three lists in Python, each of which represents a vector. The lists `d1` and `s1` represent the difference of `v2` and the sum `v2`, respectively. The number `p1` represents the "inner product" (also called the "dot product") of `v3` and `v2`. The output from Listing 3.6 is here:

```
Initial Vectors
v1: [1, 2, 3]
v2: [1, 2, 3]
v3: [5, 5, 5]
After operations
d1: [4, 3, 2]
s1: [6, 7, 8]
p1: 30
```

## WORKING WITH MATRICES

A two-dimensional matrix is a two-dimensional array of values, and you can easily create such a matrix. For example, the following code block illustrates how to access different elements in a 2D matrix:

```
mm = [["a","b","c"],["d","e","f"],["g","h","i"]];
print 'mm:       ',mm
print 'mm[0]:    ',mm[0]
print 'mm[0][1]:',mm[0][1]
```

The output from the preceding code block is here:

```
mm:         [['a', 'b', 'c'], ['d', 'e', 'f'], ['g', 'h', 'i']]
mm[0]:      ['a', 'b', 'c']
mm[0][1]: b
```

Listing 3.7 displays the contents of `My2DMatrix.py` that illustrates how to create and populate 2 two-dimensional matrix.

***LISTING 3.7: My2DMatrix.py***

```
rows = 3
cols = 3

my2DMatrix = [[0 for i in range(rows)] for j in
range(rows)]
print('Before:',my2DMatrix)

for row in range(rows):
  for col in range(cols):
    my2DMatrix[row][col] = row*row+col*col
print('After: ',my2DMatrix)
```

Listing 3.7 initializes the variables rows and cols and then uses them to create the `rows x cols` matrix `my2DMatrix` whose values are initially 0. The next part of Listing 3.7 contains a nested loop that initializes the element of `my2DMatrix` whose position is `(row,col)` with the value `row*row+col*col`. The last line of code in Listing 3.7 prints the contents of `my2DArray`. The output from Listing 3.7 is here:

```
Before: [[0, 0, 0], [0, 0, 0], [0, 0, 0]]
After:  [[0, 1, 4], [1, 2, 5], [4, 5, 8]]
```

## THE `NumPy` LIBRARY FOR MATRICES

The `NumPy` library (which you can install via `pip`) has a matrix object for manipulating matrices in `Python`. The following examples illustrate some of the features of `NumPy`.

Initialize a matrix `m` and then display its contents:

```
>>> import numpy as np
>>> m = np.matrix([[1,-2,3],[0,4,5],[7,8,-9]])
>>> m
matrix([[1, -2, 3],
        [0,  4,  5],
        [7,  8, -9]])
```

The next snippet returns the transpose of matrix `m`:

```
>>> m.T
matrix([[1, 0, 7],
        [-2,  4,  8],
        [3,  5, -9]])
```

The next snippet returns the inverse of matrix m (if it exists):

```
>>> m.I
matrix([[ 0.33043478, -0.02608696, 0.09565217],
        [-0.15217391,  0.13043478,  0.02173913],
        [ 0.12173913,  0.09565217, -0.0173913 ]])
```

The next snippet defines a vector y and then computes the product m*v:

```
>>> v = np.matrix([[2],[3],[4]])
>>> v
matrix([[2],[3],[4]])
>>> m * v
matrix([[ 8],[32],[ 2]])
```

The next snippet imports the numpy.linalg subpackage and then computes the determinant of the matrix m:

```
>>> import numpy.linalg
>>> numpy.linalg.det(m)
-229.99999999999983
```

The next snippet finds the eigenvalues of the matrix m:

```
>>> numpy.linalg.eigvals(m)
array([-13.11474312, 2.75956154, 6.35518158])
```

The next snippet finds solutions to the equation m*x = v:

```
>>> x = numpy.linalg.solve(m, v)
>>> x
matrix([[0.96521739],
        [0.17391304],
        [0.46086957]])
```

In addition to the preceding samples, the NumPy package provides additional functionality, which you can find by performing an internet search for articles and tutorials.

## QUEUES

A queue is a FIFO (First In First Out) data structure. Thus, the oldest item in a queue is removed when a new item is added to a queue that is already full.

Earlier in the chapter you learned how to use a Python List to emulate a queue. However, there is also a queue object in Python. The following code snippets illustrate how to use a queue in Python.

```
>>> from collections import deque
>>> q = deque('',maxlen=10)
>>> for i in range(10,20):
...    q.append(i)
...
```

```
>>> print q
deque([10, 11, 12, 13, 14, 15, 16, 17, 18, 19], maxlen=10)
```

The next section shows you how to use tuples in `Python`.

## TUPLES (IMMUTABLE LISTS)

`Python` supports a data type called a *tuple* that consists of comma-separated values without brackets (square brackets are for lists, round brackets are for arrays, and curly braces are for dictionaries). Various examples of Python tuples are here:

*https://docs.python.org/3.6/tutorial/datastructures.html#tuples-and-sequences*

The following code block illustrates how to create a tuple and create new tuples from an existing type in `Python`.

Define a `Python` tuple `t` as follows:

```
>>> t = 1,'a', 2,'hello',3
>>> t
(1, 'a', 2, 'hello', 3)
```

Display the first element of t:

```
>>> t[0]
1
```

Create a tuple v containing 10, 11, and t:

```
>>> v = 10,11,t
>>> v
(10, 11, (1, 'a', 2, 'hello', 3))
```

Try modifying an element of t (which is immutable):

```
>>> t[0] = 1000
Traceback (most recent call last):
  File "<stdin>", line 1, in <module>
TypeError: 'tuple' object does not support item assignment
```

`Python` "deduplication" is useful because you can remove duplicates from a set and obtain a list, as shown here:

```
>>> lst = list(set(lst))
```

**NOTE** *The "in" operator on a list to search is O(n) whereas the "in" operator on set is O(1).*

The next section discusses `Python` sets.

## SETS

A `Python` set is an unordered collection that does not contain duplicate elements. Use curly braces or the `set()` function to create sets. Set objects support set-theoretic operations such as union, intersection, and difference.

**NOTE** *`Set()` is required in order to create an empty set because `{}` creates an empty dictionary.*

The following code block illustrates how to work with a `Python` set.

Create a list of elements:

```
>>> l = ['a', 'b', 'a', 'c']
```

Create a set from the preceding list:

```
>>> s = set(l)
>>> s
set(['a', 'c', 'b'])
```

Test if an element is in the set:

```
>>> 'a' in s
True
>>> 'd' in s
False
>>>
```

Create a set from a string:

```
>>> n = set('abacad')
>>> n
set(['a', 'c', 'b', 'd'])
>>>
```

Subtract n from s:

```
>>> s - n
set([])
```

Subtract s from n:

```
>>> n - s
set(['d'])
>>>
```

The union of s and n:

```
>>> s | n
set(['a', 'c', 'b', 'd'])
```

The intersection of s and n:

```
>>> s & n
set(['a', 'c', 'b'])
```

The exclusive-or of s and n:

```
>>> s ^ n
set(['d'])
```

The next section shows you how to work with Python dictionaries.

## DICTIONARIES

`Python` has a key/value structure called a "dict" that is a hash table. A `Python` dictionary (and hash tables in general) can retrieve the value of a key in constant time, regardless of the number of entries in the dictionary (and the same is true for sets). You can think of a set as essentially just the keys (not the values) of a `dict` implementation.

The contents of a `dict` can be written as a series of key:value pairs, as shown here:

```
dict1 = {key1:value1, key2:value2, ... }
```

The "empty dict" is just an empty pair of curly braces `{}`.

### Creating a Dictionary

A `Python` dictionary (or hash table) contains of colon-separated key/value bindings inside a pair of curly braces, as shown here:

```
dict1 = {}
dict1 = {'x' : 1, 'y' : 2}
```

The preceding code snippet defines `dict1` as an empty dictionary, and then adds two key/value bindings.

### Displaying the Contents of a Dictionary

You can display the contents of `dict1` with the following code:

```
>>> dict1 = {'x':1,'y':2}
>>> dict1
{'y': 2, 'x': 1}
>>> dict1['x']
1
>>> dict1['y']
2
>>> dict1['z']
Traceback (most recent call last):
  File "<stdin>", line 1, in <module>
KeyError: 'z'
```

**NOTE** *Key/value bindings for a* `dict` *and a set are not necessarily stored in the same order that you defined them.*

`Python` dictionaries also provide the `get` method in order to retrieve key values:

```
>>> dict1.get('x')
1
>>> dict1.get('y')
2
>>> dict1.get('z')
```

As you can see, the `Python get()` method returns `None` (which is displayed as an empty string) instead of an error when referencing a key that is not defined in a dictionary. You can also use `dict` comprehensions to create dictionaries from expressions, as shown here:

```
>>> {x: x**3 for x in (1, 2, 3)}
{1: 1, 2: 8, 3: 37}
```

## Checking for Keys in a Dictionary

You can easily check for the presence of a key in a Python dictionary as follows:

```
>>> 'x' in dict1
True
>>> 'z' in dict1
False
```

Use square brackets for finding or setting a value in a dictionary. For example, `dict['abc']` finds the value associated with the key `'abc'`. You can use strings, numbers, and tuples work as key values, and you can use any type as the value.

If you access a value that is not in the `dict`, Python throws a `KeyError`. Consequently, use the "in" operator to check if the key is in the `dict` dictionary. Alternatively, use `dict.get(key)` which returns the value or `None` if the key is not present. You can even use the expression `get(key, not-found-string)` to specify the value to return if a key is not found.

## Deleting Keys From a Dictionary

Launch the `Python` interpreter and enter the following commands:

```
>>> MyDict = {'x' : 5,  'y' : 7}
>>> MyDict['z'] = 13
>>> MyDict
{'y': 7, 'x': 5, 'z': 13}
>>> del MyDict['x']
>>> MyDict
{'y': 7, 'z': 13}
>>> MyDict.keys()
```

```
['y', 'z']
>>> MyDict.values()
[13, 7]
>>> 'z' in MyDict
True
```

### Iterating Through a Dictionary

The following code snippet shows you how to iterate through a dictionary:

```
MyDict = {'x' : 5,  'y' : 7, 'z' : 13}

for key, value in MyDict.iteritems():
    print key, value
```

The output from the preceding code block is here:

```
y 7
x 5
z 13
```

### Interpolating Data From a Dictionary

The % operator substitutes values from a `Python` dictionary into a string by name. Listing 3.8 contains an example of doing so.

***LISTING 3.8: InterpolateDict1.py***

```
hash = {}
hash['beverage'] = 'coffee'
hash['count'] = 3

# %d for int, %s for string
s = 'Today I drank %(count)d cups of %(beverage)s' % hash
print('s:', s)
```

The output from the preceding code block is here:

```
Today I drank 3 cups of coffee
```

## DICTIONARY FUNCTIONS AND METHODS

`Python` provides various functions and methods for a Python dictionary, such as `cmp()`, `len()`, and `str()` that compare two dictionaries, return the length of a dictionary, and display a string representation of a dictionary, respectively.

You can also manipulate the contents of a `Python` dictionary using the functions `clear()` to remove all elements, `copy()` to return a shall copy, `get()` to retrieve the value of a key, `items()` to display the (key, value) pairs of a dictionary, `keys()` to displays the keys of a dictionary, and values() to return the list of values of a dictionary.

## DICTIONARY FORMATTING

The % operator works conveniently to substitute values from a `dict` into a string by name:

```
#create a dictionary
>>> h = {}
#add a key/value pair
>>> h['item'] = 'beer'
>>> h['count'] = 4
#interpolate using %d for int, %s for string
>>> s = 'I want %(count)d bottles of %(item)s' % h
>>> s
'I want 4 bottles of beer'
```

The next section shows you how to create an ordered `Python` dictionary.

## ORDERED DICTIONARIES

Regular `Python` dictionaries iterate over key/value pairs in arbitrary order. `Python` 2.7 introduced a new `OrderedDict` class in the collections module. The `OrderedDict` API provides the same interface as regular dictionaries but iterates over keys and values in a guaranteed order depending on when a key was first inserted:

```
>>> from collections import OrderedDict
>>> d = OrderedDict([('first', 1),
...                  ('second', 2),
...                  ('third', 3)])
>>> d.items()
[('first', 1), ('second', 2), ('third', 3)]
```

If a new entry overwrites an existing entry, the original insertion position is left unchanged:

```
>>> d['second'] = 4
>>> d.items()
[('first', 1), ('second', 4), ('third', 3)]
```

Deleting an entry and reinserting it will move it to the end:

```
>>> del d['second']
>>> d['second'] = 5
>>> d.items()
[('first', 1), ('third', 3), ('second', 5)]
```

### Sorting Dictionaries

`Python` enables you to support the entries in a dictionary. For example, you can modify the code in the preceding section to display the alphabetically sorted words and their associated word count.

## Python Multidictionaries

You can define entries in a `Python` dictionary so that they reference lists or other types of `Python` structures. Listing 3.9 displays the contents of `MultiDictionary1.py` that illustrates how to define more complex dictionaries.

***LISTING 3.9: MultiDictionary1.py***

```
from collections import defaultdict

d = {'a' : [1, 2, 3], 'b' : [4, 5]}
print 'firsts:',d

d = defaultdict(list)
d['a'].append(1)
d['a'].append(2)
d['b'].append(4)
print 'second:',d

d = defaultdict(set)
d['a'].add(1)
d['a'].add(2)
d['b'].add(4)
print 'third:',d
```

Listing 3.9 starts by defining the dictionary `d` and printing its contents. The next portion of Listing 3.9 specifies a list-oriented dictionary, and then modifies the values for the keys `a` and `b`. The final portion of Listing 3.9 specifies a set-oriented dictionary, and then modifies the values for the keys `a` and `b` as well.

The output from Listing 3.9 is here:

```
first: {'a': [1, 2, 3], 'b': [4, 5]}
second: defaultdict(<type 'list'>, {'a': [1, 2], 'b': [4]})
third: defaultdict(<type 'set'>, {'a': set([1, 2]), 'b':
set([4])})
```

The next section discusses other `Python` sequence types that have not been discussed in previous sections of this chapter.

## OTHER SEQUENCE TYPES IN PYTHON

`Python` supports 7 sequence types: `str, unicode, list, tuple, bytearray, buffer,` and `xrange`.

You can iterate through a sequence and retrieve the position index and corresponding value at the same time using the `enumerate()` function.

```
>>> for i, v in enumerate(['x', 'y', 'z']):
...     print i, v
...
```

```
0 x
1 y
2 z
```

Bytearray objects are created with the built-in function bytearray(). Although buffer objects are not directly supported by Python syntax, you can create them via the built-in buffer() function.

Objects of type xrange are created with the xrange() function. An xrange object is similar to a buffer in the sense that there is no specific syntax to create them. Moreover, xrange objects do not support operations such as slicing, concatenation, or repetition.

At this point you have seen all the Python type that you will encounter in the remaining chapters of this book, so it makes sense to discuss mutable and immutable types in Python, which is the topic of the next section.

## MUTABLE AND IMMUTABLE TYPES IN PYTHON

Python represents its data as objects. Some of these objects (such as lists and dictionaries) are mutable, which means you can change their content without changing their identity. Objects such as integers, floats, strings, and tuples are objects that cannot be changed. The key point to understand is the difference between changing the value versus assigning a new value to an object; you cannot change a string but you can assign it a different value. This detail can be verified by checking the id value of an object, as shown in Listing 3.10.

***LISTING 3.10: Mutability.py***

```
s = "abc"
print('id #1:', id(s))
print('first char:', s[0])

try:
  s[0] = "o"
except:
  print('Cannot perform reassignment')

s = "xyz"
print('id #2:',id(s))
s += "uvw"
print('id #3:',id(s))
```

The output of Listing 3.10 is here:

```
id #1: 4297972672
first char: a
Cannot perform reassignment
id #2: 4299809336
id #3: 4299777872
```

Thus, a Python type is immutable if its value cannot be changed (even though it's possible to assign a new value to such a type), otherwise a Python type is mutable. The Python immutable objects are of type bytes, complex, float, int, str, or tuple. On the other hand, dictionaries, lists, and sets are mutable. The key in a hash table must be an immutable type.

Since strings are immutable in Python, you cannot insert a string in the "middle" of a given text string unless you construct a second string using concatenation. For example, suppose you have the string:

```
"this is a string"
```

and you want to create the following string:

```
"this is a longer string"
```

The following Python code block illustrates how to perform this task:

```
text1 = "this is a string"
text2 = text1[0:10] + "longer" + text1[9:]
print 'text1:',text1
print 'text2:',text2
```

The output of the preceding code block is here:

```
text1: this is a string
text2: this is a longer string
```

## THE type() FUNCTION

The type() primitive returns the type of any object, including Python primitives, functions, and user-defined objects. The following code sample displays the type of an integer and a string:

```
var1 = 123
var2 = 456.78
print "type var1: ",type(var1)
print "type var2: ",type(var2)
```

The output of the preceding code block is here:

```
type var1:  <type 'int'>
type var2:  <type 'float'>
```

## SUMMARY

This chapter showed you how to work with various Python data structures. In particular, you learned about tuples, sets, and dictionaries. Next you learned how to work with lists and how to use list-related operations to extract sublists. In addition, you learned how to work with dictionaries, tuples, and sets in Python.

CHAPTER 4

# *Introduction to NumPy and Pandas*

The first half of this chapter starts with a quick introduction to the `Python NumPy` package, followed by a quick introduction to `Pandas` and some of its useful features. The `Pandas` package for `Python` provides a rich and powerful set of APIs for managing datasets. These APIs are very useful for machine learning and deep learning tasks that involve dynamically "slicing and dicing" subsets of datasets.

The first section contains examples of working arrays in `NumPy`, and contrasts some of the APIs for lists with the same APIs for arrays. In addition, you will see how easy it is to compute the exponent-related values (square, cube, and so forth) of elements in an array.

The second section introduces subranges, which are very useful (and frequently used) for extracting portions of datasets in machine learning tasks. In particular, you will see code samples that handle negative (−1) subranges for vectors as well as for arrays, because they are interpreted one way for vectors and a different way for arrays.

The third part of this chapter delves into other `NumPy` methods, including the `reshape()` method, which is extremely useful (and very common) when working with images files: some `TensorFlow` APIs require converting a 2D array of `(R,G,B)` values into a corresponding one-dimensional vector.

The fourth part of this chapter briefly describes `Pandas` and some of its useful features. This section contains code samples that illustrate some nice features of `DataFrames` and a brief discussion of series, which are two of the main features of `Pandas`. The second part of this chapter discusses various types of `DataFrames` that you can create, such as numeric and Boolean `DataFrames`. In addition, you will see examples of creating `DataFrames` with `NumPy` functions and random numbers.

The fifth section of this chapter shows you how to manipulate the contents of `DataFrames` with various operations. In particular, you will also see code samples that illustrate how to create `Pandas DataFrames` from `CSV` files, Excel spreadsheets, and data that is retrieved from a URL. The third section of this chapter gives you an overview of important data cleaning tasks that you can perform with `Pandas` APIs.

## WHAT IS NumPy?

`NumPy` is a `Python` library that provides many convenience methods and also better performance. `NumPy` provides a core library for scientific computing in `Python`, with performant multidimensional arrays and good vectorized math functions, along with support for linear algebra and random numbers.

`NumPy` is modeled after MatLab, with support for lists, arrays, and so forth. `NumPy` is easier to use than Matlab, and it's common in TensorFlow code as well as `Python` code.

### Useful NumPy Features

The `NumPy` package provides the *ndarray* object that encapsulates *multi-*dimensional arrays of homogeneous data types. Many `ndarray` operations are performed in compiled code in order to improve performance.

Keep in mind the following important differences between `NumPy arrays` and the standard Python sequences:

- NumPy arrays have a fixed size, whereas Python lists can expand dynamically. Whenever you modify the size of an *ndarray*, a new array is created and the original array is deleted.
- NumPy arrays are homogeneous, which means that the elements in a NumPy array must have the same data type. Except for NumPy arrays of objects, the elements in NumPy arrays of any other data type must have the same size in memory.
- NumPy arrays support more efficient execution (and require less code) of various types of operations on large numbers of data.
- Many scientific Python-based packages rely on NumPy arrays, and knowledge of NumPy arrays is becoming increasingly important.

Now that you have a general idea about `NumPy`, let's delve into some examples that illustrate how to work with `NumPy arrays`, which is the topic of the next section.

## WHAT ARE NumPy ARRAYS?

An *array* is a set of consecutive memory locations used to store data. Each item in the array is called an *element*. The number of elements in an array is called the *dimension* of the array. A typical array declaration is shown here:

```
arr1 = np.array([1,2,3,4,5])
```

The preceding code snippet declares `arr1` as an array of five elements, which you can access via `arr1[0]` through `arr1[4]`. Notice that the first element has an index value of 0, the second element has an index value of 1, and so forth. Thus, if you declare an array of 100 elements, then the 100th element has index value of 99.

**NOTE** *The first position in a* `NumPy array` *has index 0.*

`NumPy` treats arrays as vectors. Math ops are performed element-by-element. Remember the following difference: "doubling" an array *multiplies* each element by 2, whereas "doubling" a list *appends* a list to itself.

Listing 4.1 displays the contents of `nparray1.py` that illustrates some operations on a `NumPy array`.

***LISTING 4.1: nparray1.py***

```
import numpy as np

list1 = [1,2,3,4,5]
print(list1)

arr1  = np.array([1,2,3,4,5])
print(arr1)

list2 = [(1,2,3),(4,5,6)]
print(list2)

arr2  = np.array([(1,2,3),(4,5,6)])
print(arr2)
```

Listing 4.1 defines the variables `list1` and `list2` (which are Python lists), as well as the variables `arr1` and `arr2` (which are arrays), and prints their values. The output from launching Listing 4.1 is here:

```
[1, 2, 3, 4, 5]
[1 2 3 4 5]
[(1, 2, 3), (4, 5, 6)]
[[1 2 3]
 [4 5 6]]
```

As you can see, Python lists and arrays are very easy to define, and now we're ready to look at some loop operations for lists and arrays.

## WORKING WITH LOOPS

Listing 4.2 displays the contents of `loop1.py` that illustrates how to iterate through the elements of a `NumPy array` and a Python list.

***LISTING 4.2: loop1.py***

```
import numpy as np

list = [1,2,3]
arr1 = np.array([1,2,3])

for e in list:
  print(e)

for e in arr1:
  print(e)

list1 = [1,2,3,4,5]
```

Listing 4.2 initializes the variable `list`, which is a Python list, and also the variable `arr1`, which is a `NumPy array`. The next portion of Listing 4.2 contains two loops, each of which iterates through the elements in `list` and `arr1`. As you can see, the syntax is identical in both loops. The output from launching Listing 4.2 is here:

```
1
2
3
1
2
3
```

## APPENDING ELEMENTS TO ARRAYS (1)

Listing 4.3 displays the contents of `append1.py` that illustrates how to append elements to a `NumPy array` and a `Python` list.

***LISTING 4.3: append1.py***

```
import numpy as np

arr1 = np.array([1,2,3])

# these do not work:
#arr1.append(4)
#arr1 = arr1 + [5]

arr1 = np.append(arr1,4)
arr1 = np.append(arr1,[5])

for e in arr1:
  print(e)

arr2 = arr1 + arr1

for e in arr2:
  print(e)
```

Listing 4.3 initializes the variable `list`, which is a `Python` list, and also the variable `arr1`, which is a `NumPy array`. The output from launching Listing 4.3 is here:

```
1
2
3
4
5
2
4
6
8
10
```

## APPENDING ELEMENTS TO ARRAYS (2)

Listing 4.4 displays the contents of `append2.py` that illustrates how to append elements to a `NumPy array` and a `Python` list.

***LISTING 4.4: append2.py***

```
import numpy as np

arr1 = np.array([1,2,3])
arr1 = np.append(arr1,4)

for e in arr1:
  print(e)

arr1 = np.array([1,2,3])
arr1 = np.append(arr1,4)

arr2 = arr1 + arr1

for e in arr2:
  print(e)
```

Listing 4.4 initializes the variable `arr1`, which is a `NumPy array`. Notice that `NumPy arrays` do not have an "append" method: this method is available through `NumPy` itself. Another important difference between `Python` lists and `NumPy arrays`: the "+" operator *concatenates* `Python` lists, whereas this operator *doubles* the elements in a `NumPy array`. The output from launching Listing 4.4 is here:

```
1
2
3
4
2
4
6
8
```

## MULTIPLY LISTS AND ARRAYS

Listing 4.5 displays the contents of `multiply1.py` that illustrates how to multiply elements in a `Python` list and a `NumPy array`.

***LISTING 4.5: multiply1.py***

```
import numpy as np

list1 = [1,2,3]
arr1  = np.array([1,2,3])
print('list:  ',list1)
print('arr1:  ',arr1)
print('2*list:',2*list)
print('2*arr1:',2*arr1)
```

Listing 4.5 contains a `Python` list called list and a `NumPy array` called `arr1`. The `print()` statements display the contents of list and arr1 as well as the result of doubling `list1` and `arr1`. Recall that "doubling" a Python list is different from doubling a `Python` array, which you can see in the output from launching Listing 4.5:

```
('list:   ', [1, 2, 3])
('arr1:   ', array([1, 2, 3]))
('2*list:', [1, 2, 3, 1, 2, 3])
('2*arr1:', array([2, 4, 6]))
```

## DOUBLING THE ELEMENTS IN A LIST

Listing 4.6 displays the contents of `double_list1.py` that illustrates how to double the elements in a `Python` list.

***LISTING 4.6: double_list1.py***

```
import numpy as np

list1 = [1,2,3]
list2 = []

for e in list1:
  list2.append(2*e)

print('list1:',list1)
print('list2:',list2)
```

Listing 4.6 contains a `Python` list called `list1` and an empty `NumPy list` called `list2`. The next code snippet iterates through the elements of `list1` and appends them to the variable `list2`. The pair of `print()` statements display the contents of `list1` and `list2` to show you that they are the same. The output from launching Listing 4.6 is here:

```
('list: ', [1, 2, 3])
('list2:', [2, 4, 6])
```

## LISTS AND EXPONENTS

Listing 4.7 displays the contents of `exponent_list1.py` that illustrates how to compute exponents of the elements in a `Python` list.

***LISTING 4.7: exponent_list1.py***

```
import numpy as np

list1 = [1,2,3]
list2 = []

for e in list1:
  list2.append(e*e) # e*e = squared

print('list1:',list1)
print('list2:',list2)
```

Listing 4.7 contains a `Python` list called `list1` and an empty `NumPy list` called `list2`. The next code snippet iterates through the elements of `list1` and appends the square of each element to the variable `list2`. The pair of `print()` statements display the contents of `list1` and `list2`. The output from launching Listing 4.7 is here:

```
('list1:', [1, 2, 3])
('list2:', [1, 4, 9])
```

## ARRAYS AND EXPONENTS

Listing 4.8 displays the contents of `exponent_array1.py` that illustrates how to compute exponents of the elements in a `NumPy array`.

***LISTING 4.8: exponent_array1.py***

```
import numpy as np

arr1 = np.array([1,2,3])
arr2 = arr1**2
arr3 = arr1**3

print('arr1:',arr1)
print('arr2:',arr2)
print('arr3:',arr3)
```

Listing 4.8 contains a `NumPy array` called `arr1` followed by two `NumPy arrays` called `arr2` and `arr3`. Notice the compact manner in which the `NumPy arr2` is initialized with the square of the elements in `arr1`, followed by the initialization of the `NumPy array arr3` with the cube of the elements in `arr1`. The three `print()` statements display the contents of `arr1`, `arr2`, and `arr3`. The output from launching Listing 4.8 is here:

```
('arr1:', array([1, 2, 3]))
('arr2:', array([1, 4, 9]))
('arr3:', array([1, 8, 27]))
```

## MATH OPERATIONS AND ARRAYS

Listing 4.9 displays the contents of `mathops_array1.py` that illustrates how to compute exponents of the elements in a `NumPy array`.

***LISTING 4.9: mathops_array1.py***

```
import numpy as np

arr1 = np.array([1,2,3])
sqrt = np.sqrt(arr1)
log1 = np.log(arr1)
exp1 = np.exp(arr1)

print('sqrt:',sqrt)
print('log1:',log1)
print('exp1:',exp1)
```

Listing 4.9 contains a `NumPy array` called `arr1` followed by three `NumPy arrays` called `sqrt`, `log1`, and `exp1` that are initialized with the square root, the log, and the exponential value of the elements in `arr1`, respectively. The three `print()` statements display the contents of `sqrt`, `log1`, and `exp1`. The output from launching Listing 4.9 is here:

```
('sqrt:', array([1.        , 1.41421356, 1.73205081]))
('log1:', array([0.        , 0.69314718, 1.09861229]))
('exp1:', array([2.71828183, 7.3890561,  20.08553692]))
```

## WORKING WITH "–1" SUBRANGES WITH VECTORS

Listing 4.10 displays the contents of `npsubarray2.py` that illustrates how to compute exponents of the elements in a `NumPy array`.

***LISTING 4.10: npsubarray2.py***

```
import numpy as np

# -1 => "all except the last element in ..." (row or col)
```

```
arr1  = np.array([1,2,3,4,5])
print('arr1:',arr1)
print('arr1[0:-1]:',arr1[0:-1])
print('arr1[1:-1]:',arr1[1:-1])
print('arr1[::-1]:', arr1[::-1]) # reverse!
```

Listing 4.10 contains a `NumPy array` called `arr1` followed by four `print` statements, each of which displays a different subrange of values in `arr1`. The output from launching Listing 4.10 is here:

```
('arr1:',       array([1, 2, 3, 4, 5]))
('arr1[0:-1]:', array([1, 2, 3, 4]))
('arr1[1:-1]:', array([2, 3, 4]))
('arr1[::-1]:', array([5, 4, 3, 2, 1]))
```

## WORKING WITH "–1" SUBRANGES WITH ARRAYS

Listing 4.11 displays the contents of `np2darray2.py` that illustrates how to compute exponents of the elements in a `NumPy array`.

### *LISTING 4.11: np2darray2.py*

```
import numpy as np

# -1 => "the last element in ..." (row or col)

arr1  = np.array([(1,2,3),(4,5,6),(7,8,9),(10,11,12)])
print('arr1:',         arr1)
print('arr1[-1,:]:',   arr1[-1,:])
print('arr1[:,-1]:',   arr1[:,-1])
print('arr1[-1:,-1]:',arr1[-1:,-1])
```

Listing 4.11 contains a `NumPy array` called `arr1` followed by four `print` statements, each of which displays a different subrange of values in `arr1`. The output from launching Listing 4.11 is here:

```
(arr1:', array([[1,  2,  3],
                 [4,  5,  6],
                 [7,  8,  9],
                 [10, 11, 12]]))
(arr1[-1,:]]',   array([10, 11, 12]))
(arr1[:,-1]:',   array([3,  6,  9, 12]))
(arr1[-1:,-1]]', array([12]))
```

## OTHER USEFUL NumPy METHODS

In addition to the `NumPy` methods that you saw in the code samples prior to this section, the following (often intuitively-named) `NumPy` methods are also very useful.

- The method np.zeros() initializes an array with 0 values.
- The method np.ones() initializes an array with 1 values.

- The method np.empty()initializes an array with 0 values.
- The method np.arange() provides a range of numbers.
- The method np.shape() displays the shape of an object.
- The method np.reshape() <= *very useful!*.
- The method np.linspace() <= *useful in regression*.
- The method np.mean() computes the mean of a set of numbers.
- The method np.std() computes the standard deviation of a set of numbers.

Although the `np.zeros()` and `np.empty()` both initialize a 2D array with 0, `np.zeros()` requires less execution time. You could also use `np.full(size, 0)`, but this method is the slowest of all three methods.

The `reshape()` method and the `linspace()` method are very useful for changing the dimensions of an array and generating a list of numeric values, respectively. The `reshape()` method often appears in TensorFlow code, and the `linspace()` method is useful for generating a set of numbers in linear regression.

The `mean()` and `std()` methods are useful for calculating the mean and the standard deviation of a set of numbers. For example, you can use these two methods in order to resize the values in a Gaussian distribution so that their mean is 0 and the standard deviation is 1. This process is called *standardizing* a Gaussian distribution.

## ARRAYS AND VECTOR OPERATIONS

Listing 4.12 displays the contents of `array_vector.py` that illustrates how to perform vector operations on the elements in a `NumPy array`.

***LISTING 4.12: array_vector.py***

```
import numpy as np

a = np.array([[1,2], [3, 4]])
b = np.array([[5,6], [7,8]])

print('a:          ', a)
print('b:          ', b)
print('a + b:      ', a+b)
print('a - b:      ', a-b)
print('a * b:      ', a*b)
print('a / b:      ', a/b)
print('b / a:      ', b/a)
print('a.dot(b):',a.dot(b))
```

Listing 4.12 contains two `NumPy arrays` called `a` and `b` followed by eight `print` statements, each of which displays the result of "applying" a different arithmetic operation to the NumPy arrays a and b. The output from launching Listing 4.12 is here:

```
('a     :   ', array([[1, 2], [3, 4]]))
('b     :   ', array([[5, 6], [7, 8]]))
('a + b:    ', array([[ 6,  8], [10, 12]]))
('a - b:    ', array([[-4, -4], [-4, -4]]))
('a * b:    ', array([[ 5, 12], [21, 32]]))
('a / b:    ', array([[0, 0], [0, 0]]))
('b / a:    ', array([[5, 3], [2, 2]]))
('a.dot(b):', array([[19, 22], [43, 50]]))
```

## NUMPY AND DOT PRODUCTS (1)

Listing 4.13 displays the contents of dotproduct1.py that illustrates how to perform the dot product on the elements in a NumPy array.

***LISTING 4.13: dotproduct1.py***

```
import numpy as np

a = np.array([1,2])
b = np.array([2,3])

dot2 = 0
for e,f in zip(a,b):
  dot2 += e*f

print('a:    ',a)
print('b:    ',b)
print('a*b: ',a*b)
print('dot1:',a.dot(b))
print('dot2:',dot2)
```

Listing 4.13 contains two NumPy arrays called a and b followed by a simple loop that computes the dot product of a and b. The next section contains five print statements that display the contents of a and b, their inner product that's calculated in three different ways. The output from launching Listing 4.13 is here:

```
('a:    ', array([1, 2]))
('b:    ', array([2, 3]))
('a*b: ', array([2, 6]))
('dot1:', 8)
('dot2:', 8)
```

## NUMPY AND DOT PRODUCTS (2)

NumPy arrays support a "dot" method for calculating the inner product of an array of numbers, which uses the same formula that you use for calculating the inner product of a pair of vectors. Listing 4.14 displays the contents of `dotproduct2.py` that illustrates how to calculate the dot product of two `NumPy arrays`.

***LISTING 4.14: dotproduct2.py***

```
import numpy as np

a = np.array([1,2])
b = np.array([2,3])

print('a:           ',a)
print('b:           ',b)
print('a.dot(b):    ',a.dot(b))
print('b.dot(a):    ',b.dot(a))
print('np.dot(a,b):',np.dot(a,b))
print('np.dot(b,a):',np.dot(b,a))
```

Listing 4.14 contains two `NumPy arrays` called `a` and `b` followed by six `print` statements that display the contents of `a` and `b`, and also their inner product that's calculated in three different ways. The output from launching Listing 4.14 is here:

```
('a:           ', array([1, 2]))
('b:           ', array([2, 3]))
('a.dot(b):    ', 8)
('b.dot(a):    ', 8)
('np.dot(a,b):', 8)
('np.dot(b,a):', 8)
```

## NUMPY AND THE "NORM" OF VECTORS

The "norm" of a vector (or an array of numbers) is the length of a vector, which is the square root of the dot product of a vector with itself. `NumPy` also provides the "sum" and "square" functions that you can use to calculate the norm of a vector.

Listing 4.15 displays the contents of `array_norm.py` that illustrates how to calculate the magnitude ("norm") of a `NumPy array` of numbers.

***LISTING 4.15: array_norm.py***

```
import numpy as np

a = np.array([2,3])
asquare = np.square(a)
asqsum  = np.sum(np.square(a))
anorm1  = np.sqrt(np.sum(a*a))
anorm2  = np.sqrt(np.sum(np.square(a)))
anorm3  = np.linalg.norm(a)
```

```
print('a:      ',a)
print('asquare:',asquare)
print('asqsum: ',asqsum)
print('anorm1: ',anorm1)
print('anorm2: ',anorm2)
print('anorm3: ',anorm3)
```

Listing 4.15 contains an initial `NumPy array` called `a`, followed by the `NumPy array` `asquare` and the numeric values `asqsum`, `anorm1`, `anorm2`, and `anorm3`. The `NumPy array` `asquare` contains the square of the elements in the `NumPy array` `a`, and the numeric value `asqsum` contains the sum of the elements in the `NumPy array` `asquare`.

Next, the numeric value `anorm1` equals the square root of the sum of the square of the elements in a. The numeric value `anorm2` is the same as `anorm1`, computed in a slightly different fashion. Finally, the numeric value `anorm3` is equal to `anorm2`, but as you can see, `anorm3` is calculated via a single `NumPy` method, whereas `anorm2` requires a succession of `NumPy` methods.

The last portion of Listing 4.15 consists of six `print()` statements, each of which displays the computed values. The output from launching Listing 4.15 is here:

```
('a:      ', array([2, 3]))
('asquare:', array([4, 9]))
('asqsum: ', 13)
('anorm1: ', 3.605551275463989)
('anorm2: ', 3.605551275463989)
('anorm3: ', 3.605551275463989)
```

## NUMPY AND OTHER OPERATIONS

`NumPy` provides the "*" operator to multiply the components of two vectors to produce a third vector whose components are the products of the corresponding components of the initial pair of vectors. This operation is called a Hadamard product, named after French mathematician Jacques Hadamard. If you then add the components of the third vector, the sum is equal to the inner product of the initial pair of vectors.

Listing 4.16 displays the contents of `otherops.py` that illustrates how to perform other operations on a `NumPy array`.

### *LISTING 4.16: otherops.py*

```
import numpy as np

a = np.array([1,2])
b = np.array([3,4])

print('a:          ',a)
print('b:          ',b)
```

```
print('a*b:           ',a*b)
print('np.sum(a*b): ',np.sum(a*b))
print('(a*b.sum()): ', (a*b).sum())
```

Listing 4.16 contains two NumPy arrays called a and b followed five print statements that display the contents of a and b, their Hadamard product, and also their inner product that's calculated in two different ways. The output from launching Listing 4.16 is here:

```
('a:           ', array([1, 2]))
('b:           ', array([3, 4]))
('a*b:         ', array([3, 8]))
('np.sum(a*b): ', 11)
('(a*b.sum()): ', 11)
```

## NUMPY AND THE RESHAPE() METHOD

NumPy arrays support the "reshape" method that enables you to restructure the dimensions of an array of numbers. In general, if a NumPy array contains m elements, where m is a positive integer, then that array can be restructured as an m1 x m2 NumPy array, where m1 and m2 are positive integers such that m1*m2 = m.

Listing 4.17 displays the contents of numpy_reshape.py that illustrates how to use the reshape() method on a NumPy array.

***LISTING 4.17: numpy_reshape.py***

```
import numpy as np

x = np.array([[2, 3], [4, 5], [6, 7]])
print(x.shape) # (3, 2)

x = x.reshape((2, 3))
print(x.shape) # (2, 3)
print('x1:',x)

x = x.reshape((-1))
print(x.shape) # (6,)
print('x2:',x)

x = x.reshape((6, -1))
print(x.shape) # (6, 1)
print('x3:',x)

x = x.reshape((-1, 6))
print(x.shape) # (1, 6)
print('x4:',x)
```

Listing 4.17 contains a NumPy array called x whose dimensions are 3x2, followed by a set of invocations of the reshape() method that reshape the contents of x. The first invocation of the reshape() method changes the shape of x from 3x2 to 2x3. The second invocation changes the shape of x from 2x3 to 6x1. The third invocation changes the shape of x from 1x6 to 6x1. The final invocation changes the shape of x from 6x1 to 1x6 again.

Each invocation of the `reshape()` method is followed by a `print()` statement so that you can see the effect of the invocation. The output from launching Listing 4.17 is here:

```
(3, 2)
(2, 3)
('x1:', array([[2, 3, 4],
       [5, 6, 7]]))
(6,)
('x2:', array([2, 3, 4, 5, 6, 7]))
(6, 1)
('x3:', array([[2],
       [3],
       [4],
       [5],
       [6],
       [7]]))
(1, 6)
```

## CALCULATING THE MEAN AND STANDARD DEVIATION

If you need to review these concepts from statistics (and perhaps also the mean, median, and mode as well), please read the appropriate on-line tutorials.

`NumPy` provides various built-in functions that perform statistical calculations, such as the following list of methods:

```
np.linspace() <= useful for regression
np.mean()
np.std()
```

The `np.linspace()` method generates a set of equally spaced numbers between a lower bound and an upper bound. The `np.mean()` and `np.std()` methods calculate the mean and standard deviation, respectively, of a set of numbers. Listing 4.18 displays the contents of `sample_mean_std.py` that illustrates how to calculate statistical values from a `NumPy array`.

***LISTING 4.18: sample_mean_std.py***

```
import numpy as np

x2 = np.arange(8)
print 'mean = ',x2.mean()
print 'std  = ',x2.std()

x3 = (x2 - x2.mean())/x2.std()
print 'x3 mean = ',x3.mean()
print 'x3 std  = ',x3.std()
```

Listing 4.18 contains a NumPy array x2 that consists of the first eight integers. Next, the mean() and std() that are "associated" with x2 are invoked in order to calculate the mean and standard deviation, respectively, of the elements of x2. The output from launching Listing 4.18 is here:

```
('a:            ', array([1, 2]))
('b:            ', array([3, 4]))
```

## CALCULATING MEAN AND STANDARD DEVIATION

The code sample in this section extends the code sample in the previous section with additional statistical values, and the code in Listing 4.19 can be used for any data distribution. Keep in mind that the code sample uses random numbers simply for the purposes of illustration: after you have launched the code sample, replace those numbers with values from a CSV file or some other dataset containing meaningful values.

Moreover, this section does not provide details regarding the meaning of quartiles, but you can learn about quartiles here: *https://en.wikipedia.org/wiki/Quartile*

Listing 4.19 displays the contents of stat_summary.py that illustrates how to display various statistical values from a NumPy array of random numbers.

***LISTING 4.19: stat_values.py***

```
import numpy as np

from numpy import percentile
from numpy.random import rand

# generate data sample
data = np.random.rand(1000)

# calculate quartiles, min, and max
quartiles = percentile(data, [25, 50, 75])
data_min, data_max = data.min(), data.max()

# print summary information
print('Minimum:  %.3f' % data_min)
print('Q1 value: %.3f' % quartiles[0])
print('Median:   %.3f' % quartiles[1])
print('Mean Val: %.3f' % data.mean())
print('Std Dev:  %.3f' % data.std())
print('Q3 value: %.3f' % quartiles[2])
print('Maximum:  %.3f' % data_max)
```

The data sample (shown in bold) in Listing 4.19 is from a uniform distribution between 0 and 1. The NumPy percentile() function calculates a linear interpolation (average) between observations, which is needed to calculate the median on a sample with an even number of values. As you can surmise, the

NumPy functions min() and max() calculate the smallest and largest values in the data sample. The output from launching Listing 4.19 is here:

```
Minimum:   0.000
Q1 value: 0.237
Median:    0.500
Mean Val: 0.495
Std Dev:   0.295
Q3 value: 0.747
Maximum:   0.999
```

This concludes the portion of the chapter pertaining to NumPy. The second half of this chapter discusses some of the features of Pandas.

## WHAT IS PANDAS?

Pandas is a Python package that is compatible with other Python packages, such as NumPy, Matplotlib, and so forth. Install Pandas by opening a command shell and invoking this command for Python 3.x:

```
pip3 install pandas
```

In many ways the Pandas package has the semantics of a spreadsheet, and it also works with xsl, xml, html, csv file types. Pandas provides a data type called a DataFrame (similar to a Python dictionary) with extremely powerful functionality, which is discussed in the next section.

Pandas DataFrames support a variety of input types, such as ndarrays, lists, dicts, or Series. Pandas also provides another data type called Pandas Series (not discussed in this chapter), this data structure provides another mechanism for managing data (search online for more details).

### Pandas DataFrames

In simplified terms, a Pandas DataFrame is a two-dimensional data structure, and it's convenient to think of the data structure in terms of rows and columns. DataFrames can be labeled (rows as well as columns), and the columns can contain different data types.

By way of analogy, it might be useful to think of a DataFrame as the counterpart to a spreadsheet, which makes it a very useful data type in Pandas-related Python scripts. The source of the dataset can be a data file, database tables, web service, and so forth. Pandas DataFrame features include:

- dataframe methods
- dataframe statistics
- grouping, pivoting, and reshaping
- dealing with missing data
- joining dataframes

## Dataframes and Data Cleaning Tasks

The specific tasks that you need to perform depend on the structure and contents of a dataset. In general, you will perform a workflow with the following steps (not necessarily always in this order), all of which can be performed with a `Pandas DataFrame`:

- Read data into a dataframe.
- Display top of dataframe.
- Display column data types.
- Display non-missing values.
- Replace NA with a value.
- Iterate through the columns.
- Include statistics for each column.
- Find missing values.
- Total missing values.
- Find the percentage of missing values.
- Sort table values.
- Print summary information.
- Find columns with > 50% missing values
- Rename columns.

# A LABELED PANDAS DATAFRAME

Listing 4.20 displays the contents of `pandas_labeled_df.py` that illustrates how to define a `Pandas DataFrame` whose rows and columns are labeled.

***LISTING 4.20: pandas_labeled_df.py***

```
import numpy
import pandas

myarray = numpy.array([[10,30,20], [50,40,60],[1000,2000,3000]])

rownames = ['apples', 'oranges', 'beer']
colnames = ['January', 'February', 'March']

mydf = Pandas.DataFrame(myarray, index=rownames,
columns=colnames)

print(mydf)
print(mydf.describe())
```

Listing 4.20 contains two important statements followed by the variable `myarray`, which is a 3x3 `NumPy array` of numbers. The variables `rownames` and `colnames` provide names for the rows and columns, respectively, of the data in `myarray`. Next, the variable `mydf` is initialized as a `Pandas DataFrame` with the specified datasource (i.e., `myarray`).

You might be surprised to see that the first portion of the following output requires a single `print` statement (which simply displays the contents of `mydf`). The second portion of the output is generated by invoking the `describe()` method that is available for any `NumPy DataFrame`. The `describe()` method is very useful: you will see various statistical quantities, such as the mean, standard deviation minimum, and maximum performed `column_wise` (not `row_wise`), along with values for the 25th, 50th, and 75th percentiles. The output of Listing 4.20 is here:

```
         January  February  March
apples        10        30     20
oranges       50        40     60
beer        1000      2000   3000
           January      February        March
count     3.000000      3.000000     3.000000
mean    353.333333    690.000000  1026.666667
std     560.386771   1134.504297  1709.073823
min      10.000000     30.000000    20.000000
25%      30.000000     35.000000    40.000000
50%      50.000000     40.000000    60.000000
75%     525.000000   1020.000000  1530.000000
max    1000.000000   2000.000000  3000.000000
```

## PANDAS NUMERIC DATAFRAMES

Listing 4.21 displays the contents of `pandas_numeric_df.py` that illustrates how to define a `Pandas DataFrame` whose rows and columns are numbers (but the column labels are characters).

***LISTING 4.21: pandas_numeric_df.py***

```
import pandas as pd

df1 = pd.DataFrame(np.random.randn(10, 4),
columns=['A','B','C','D'])
df2 = pd.DataFrame(np.random.randn(7, 3),
columns=['A','B','C'])
df3 = df1 + df2
```

The essence of Listing 4.21 involves initializing the `DataFrames` `df1` and `df2`, and then defining the `DataFrame` `df3` as the sum of `df1` and `df2`. The output from Listing 4.21 is here:

```
        A       B       C   D
0  0.0457 -0.0141  1.3809 NaN
1 -0.9554 -1.5010  0.0372 NaN
2 -0.6627  1.5348 -0.8597 NaN
3 -2.4529  1.2373 -0.1337 NaN
4  1.4145  1.9517 -2.3204 NaN
```

```
5 -0.4949 -1.6497 -1.0846 NaN
6 -1.0476 -1.7486 -0.8055 NaN
7     NaN     NaN     NaN NaN
8     NaN     NaN     NaN NaN
9     NaN     NaN     NaN NaN
```

Keep in mind that the default behavior for operations involving a `DataFrame` and `Series` is to align the `Series` index on the `DataFrame` columns; this results in a row-wise output. Here is a simple illustration:

```
names = pd.Series(['SF', 'San Jose', 'Sacramento'])
sizes = pd.Series([852469, 1015785, 485199])

df = pd.DataFrame({'Cities': names, 'Size': sizes})
df = pd.DataFrame({'City name': names,'sizes': sizes})

print(df)
```

The output of the preceding code block is here:

```
    City name    sizes
0          SF   852469
1    San Jose  1015785
2  Sacramento   485199
```

## PANDAS BOOLEAN DATAFRAMES

`Pandas` supports `Boolean` operations on `DataFrames`, such as the logical or, the logical and, and the logical negation of a pair of `DataFrames`. Listing 4.22 displays the contents of `pandas_boolean_df.py` that illustrates how to define a `Pandas DataFrame` whose rows and columns are `Boolean` values.

***LISTING 4.22: pandas_boolean_df.py***

```
import pandas as pd

df1 = pd.DataFrame({'a' : [1, 0, 1], 'b' : [0, 1, 1]},
dtype=bool)
df2 = pd.DataFrame({'a' : [0, 1, 1], 'b' : [1, 1, 0]},
dtype=bool)

print("df1 & df2:")
print(df1 & df2)

print("df1 | df2:")
print(df1 | df2)

print("df1 ^ df2:")
print(df1 ^ df2)
```

Listing 4.22 initializes the `DataFrames` `df1` and `df2`, and then computes `df1 & df2`, df1 `| df2`, `df1 ^ df2`, which represent the logical `AND`, the logical

OR, and the logical negation, respectively, of df1 and df2. The output from launching the code in Listing 4.22 is here:

```
df1 & df2:
       a      b
0  False  False
1  False   True
2   True  False
df1 | df2:
      a     b
0  True  True
1  True  True
2  True  True
df1 ^ df2:
       a      b
0   True   True
1   True  False
2  False   True
```

## Transposing a Pandas DataFrame

The T attribute (as well as the transpose function) enables you to generate the transpose of a Pandas DataFrame, similar to a NumPy ndarray.

For example, the following code snippet defines a Pandas DataFrame df1 and then displays the transpose of df1:

```
df1 = pd.DataFrame({'a' : [1, 0, 1], 'b' : [0, 1, 1]},
dtype=int)

print("df1.T:")
print(df1.T)
```

The output is here:

```
df1.T:
   0  1  2
a  1  0  1
b  0  1  1
```

The following code snippet defines Pandas DataFrames df1 and df2 and then displays their sum:

```
df1 = pd.DataFrame({'a' : [1, 0, 1], 'b' : [0, 1, 1]},
dtype=int)
df2 = pd.DataFrame({'a' : [3, 3, 3], 'b' : [5, 5, 5]},
dtype=int)

print("df1 + df2:")
print(df1 + df2)
```

The output is here:

```
df1 + df2:
   a  b
```

```
0  4  5
1  3  6
2  4  6
```

## PANDAS DATAFRAMES AND RANDOM NUMBERS

Listing 4.23 displays the contents of `pandas_random_df.py` that illustrates how to create a `Pandas DataFrame` with random numbers.

***LISTING 4.23: pandas_random_df.py***

```
import pandas as pd
import numpy as np

df = pd.DataFrame(np.random.randint(1, 5, size=(5, 2)),
columns=['a','b'])
df = df.append(df.agg(['sum', 'mean']))

print("Contents of dataframe:")
print(df)
```

Listing 4.23 defines the `Pandas DataFrame df` that consists of five rows and two columns of random integers between 1 and 5. Notice that the columns of `df` are labeled "a" and "b." In addition, the next code snippet appends two rows consisting of the sum and the mean of the numbers in both columns. The output of Listing 4.23 is here:

```
a     b
0      1.0  2.0
1      1.0  1.0
2      4.0  3.0
3      3.0  1.0
4      1.0  2.0
sum   10.0  9.0
mean   2.0  1.8
```

## COMBINING PANDAS DATAFRAMES (1)

Listing 4.24 displays the contents of `pandas_combine_df.py` that illustrates how to combine `Pandas DataFrames`.

***LISTING 4.24: pandas_combine_df.py***

```
import pandas as pd
import numpy as np

df = pd.DataFrame({'foo1' : np.random.randn(5),
                   'foo2' : np.random.randn(5)})

print("contents of df:")
print(df)
```

```
print("contents of foo1:")
print(df.foo1)

print("contents of foo2:")
print(df.foo2)
```

Listing 4.24 defines the `Pandas DataFrame df` that consists of five rows and two columns (labeled "`foo1`" and "`foo2`") of random real numbers between 0 and 5. The next portion of Listing 4.5 displays the contents of `df` and `foo1`. The output of Listing 4.24 is here:

```
contents of df:
       foo1      foo2
0  0.274680 -0.848669
1 -0.399771 -0.814679
2  0.454443 -0.363392
3  0.473753  0.550849
4 -0.211783 -0.015014
contents of foo1:
0  0.256773
1  1.204322
2  1.040515
3 -0.518414
4  0.634141
Name: foo1, dtype: float64 contents of foo2:
0 -2.506550
1 -0.896516
2 -0.222923
3  0.934574
4  0.527033
Name: foo2, dtype: float64
```

## COMBINING PANDAS DATAFRAMES (2)

`Pandas` supports the "concat" method in `DataFrames` in order to concatenate `DataFrames`. Listing 4.25 displays the contents of `concat_frames.py` that illustrates how to combine two `Pandas DataFrames`.

***LISTING 4.25: concat_frames.py***

```
import pandas as pd

can_weather = pd.DataFrame({
    "city": ["Vancouver","Toronto","Montreal"],
    "temperature": [72,65,50],
    "humidity": [40, 20, 25]
})

us_weather = pd.DataFrame({
    "city": ["SF","Chicago","LA"],
    "temperature": [60,40,85],
    "humidity": [30, 15, 55]
```

```
})

df = pd.concat([can_weather, us_weather])
print(df)
```

The first line in Listing 4.25 is an import statement, followed by the definition of the `Pandas` dataframes `can_weather` and `us_weather` that contain weather-related information for cities in Canada and the United States, respectively. The `Pandas DataFrame df` is the concatenation of `can_weather` and `us_weather`. The output from Listing 4.25 is here:

```
0  Vancouver          40            72
1    Toronto          20            65
2   Montreal          25            50
0         SF          30            60
1    Chicago          15            40
2         LA          55            85
```

## DATA MANIPULATION WITH PANDAS DATAFRAMES (1)

As a simple example, suppose that we have a two-person company that keeps track of income and expenses on a quarterly basis, and we want to calculate the profit/loss for each quarter, and also the overall profit/loss.

Listing 4.26 displays the contents of `pandas_quarterly_df1.py` that illustrates how to define a `Pandas DataFrame` consisting of income-related values.

***LISTING 4.26: pandas_quarterly_df1.py***

```
import pandas as pd

summary = {
    'Quarter': ['Q1', 'Q2', 'Q3', 'Q4'],
    'Cost':    [23500, 34000, 57000, 32000],
    'Revenue': [40000, 40000, 40000, 40000]
}

df = pd.DataFrame(summary)

print("Entire Dataset:\n",df)
print("Quarter:\n",df.Quarter)
print("Cost:\n",df.Cost)
print("Revenue:\n",df.Revenue)
```

Listing 4.26 defines the variable `summary` that contains hard-coded quarterly information about cost and revenue for our two-person company. In general these hard-coded values would be replaced by data from another source (such as a CSV file), so think of this code sample as a simple way to illustrate some of the functionality that is available in `Pandas DataFrames`.

The variable `df` is a `Pandas DataFrame` based on the data in the `summary` variable. The three `print` statements display the quarters, the cost per quarter, and the revenue per quarter.

The output from Listing 4.26 is here:

```
Entire Dataset:
     Cost Quarter  Revenue
0  23500      Q1    40000
1  34000      Q2    60000
2  57000      Q3    50000
3  32000      Q4    30000
Quarter:
 0    Q1
1    Q2
2    Q3
3    Q4
Name: Quarter, dtype: object
Cost:
 0    23500
1    34000
2    57000
3    32000
Name: Cost, dtype: int64
Revenue:
 0    40000
1    60000
2    50000
3    30000
Name: Revenue, dtype: int64
```

## DATA MANIPULATION WITH PANDAS DATAFRAMES (2)

In this section, let's suppose that we have a two-person company that keeps track of income and expenses on a quarterly basis, and we want to calculate the profit/loss for each quarter, and also the overall profit/loss.

Listing 4.27 displays the contents of `pandas_quarterly_df1.py` that illustrates how to define a `Pandas DataFrame` consisting of income-related values.

### *LISTING 4.27: pandas_quarterly_df2.py*

```
import pandas as pd

summary = {
    'Quarter': ['Q1', 'Q2', 'Q3', 'Q4'],
    'Cost':    [_23500, _34000, _57000, _32000],
    'Revenue': [40000, 40000, 40000, 40000]
}

df = pd.DataFrame(summary)
print("First Dataset:\n",df)

df['Total'] = df.sum(axis=1)
print("Second Dataset:\n",df)
```

Listing 4.27 defines the variable `summary` that contains quarterly information about cost and revenue for our two-person company. The variable `df` is a `Pandas DataFrame` based on the data in the `summary` variable. The three `print` statements display the quarters, the cost per quarter, and the revenue per quarter. The output from Listing 4.27 is here:

```
First Dataset:
     Cost Quarter  Revenue
0 -23500       Q1    40000
1 -34000       Q2    60000
2 -57000       Q3    50000
3 -32000       Q4    30000
Second Dataset:
     Cost Quarter  Revenue  Total
0 -23500       Q1    40000  16500
1 -34000       Q2    60000  26000
2 -57000       Q3    50000  -7000
3 -32000       Q4    30000  -2000
```

## DATA MANIPULATION WITH PANDAS DATAFRAMES (3)

Let's start with the same assumption as the previous section: we have a two-person company that keeps track of income and expenses on a quarterly basis, and we want to calculate the profit/loss for each quarter, and also the overall profit/loss. In addition, we want to compute column totals and row totals.

Listing 4.28 displays the contents of `pandas-quarterly-df1.py` that illustrates how to define a `Pandas DataFrame` consisting of income-related values.

***LISTING 4.28: pandas-quarterly-df3.py***

```
import pandas as pd

summary = {
    'Quarter': ['Q1', 'Q2', 'Q3', 'Q4'],
    'Cost':    [-23500, -34000, -57000, -32000],
    'Revenue': [40000, 40000, 40000, 40000]
}

df = pd.DataFrame(summary)
print("First Dataset:\n",df)

df['Total'] = df.sum(axis=1)
df.loc['Sum'] = df.sum()
print("Second Dataset:\n",df)

# or df.loc['avg'] / 3
#df.loc['avg'] = df[:3].mean()
#print("Third Dataset:\n",df)
```

Listing 4.28 defines the variable `summary` that contains quarterly information about cost and revenue for our two-person company. The variable `df` is a `Pandas DataFrame` based on the data in the `summary` variable. The three `print` statements display the quarters, the cost per quarter, and the revenue per quarter. The output from Listing 4.28 is here:

```
First Dataset:
     Cost Quarter  Revenue
0 -23500       Q1    40000
1 -34000       Q2    60000
2 -57000       Q3    50000
3 -32000       Q4    30000
Second Dataset:
         Cost   Quarter  Revenue  Total
0     -23500         Q1    40000  16500
1     -34000         Q2    60000  26000
2     -57000         Q3    50000  -7000
3     -32000         Q4    30000  -2000
Sum -146500  Q1Q2Q3Q4   180000  33500
```

## PANDAS DATAFRAMES AND CSV FILES

The code samples in several earlier sections contain hard-coded data inside the `Python` scripts. However, it's also very common to read data from a `CSV` file. You can use the `Python csv.reader()` function, the `NumPy loadtxt()` function, or the `Pandas` function `read-csv()` function (shown in this section) to read the contents of `CSV` files.

Listing 4.29 displays the contents of `weather-data.py` that illustrates how to read a `CSV` file, initialize a `Pandas DataFrame` with the contents of that `CSV` file, and display various subsets of the data in the `Pandas DataFrames`.

***LISTING 4.29: weather-data.py***

```
import pandas as pd

df = pd.read-csv("weather-data.csv")

print(df)
print(df.shape)  # rows, columns
print(df.head()) # df.head(3)
print(df.tail())
print(df[1:3])
print(df.columns)
print(type(df['day']))
print(df[['day','temperature']])
print(df['temperature'].max())
```

Listing 4.29 invokes the `Pandas read-csv()` function to read the contents of the `CSV` file `weather-data.csv`, followed by a set of `Python print()` statements that display various portions of the `CSV` file. The output from Listing 4.29 is here:

```
day,temperature,windspeed,event
7/1/2018,42,16,Rain
7/2/2018,45,3,Sunny
```

```
7/3/2018,78,12,Snow
7/4/2018,74,9,Snow
7/5/2018,42,24,Rain
7/6/2018,51,32,Sunny
```

In some situations you might need to apply Boolean conditional logic to "filter out" some rows of data, based on a conditional condition that's applied to a column value.

Listing 4.30 displays the contents of the CSV file people.csv and Listing 4.31 displays the contents of people_pandas.py that illustrates how to define a Pandas DataFrame that reads the CSV file and manipulates the data.

**_LISTING 4.30: people.csv_**

```
fname,lname,age,gender,country
john,smith,30,m,usa
jane,smith,31,f,france
jack,jones,32,f,france
dave,stone,33,f,france
sara,stein,34,f,france
eddy,bower,35,f,france
```

**_LISTING 4.31: people_pandas.py_**

```
import pandas as pd

df = pd.read_csv('people.csv')
df.info()
print('fname:')
print(df['fname'])
print('____________')
print('age over 33:')
print(df['age'] > 33)
print('____________')
print('age over 33:')
myfilter = df['age'] >  33
print(df[myfilter])
```

Listing 4.31 populate the Pandas DataFrame df with the contents of the CSV file people.csv. The next portion of Listing 4.12 displays the structure of df, followed by the first names of all the people. The next portion of Listing 4.12 displays a tabular list of six rows containing either True or False depending on whether a person is over 33 or at most 33, respectively.

The final portion of Listing 4.31 displays a tabular list of two rows containing all the details of the people who are over 33. The output from Listing 4.31 is here:

```
myfilter = df['age'] >  33
<class 'pandas.core.frame.DataFrame'>
RangeIndex: 6 entries, 0 to 5
Data columns (total 5 columns):
```

```
fname      6 non_null object
lname      6 non_null object
age        6 non_null int64
gender     6 non_null object
country    6 non_null object
dtypes: int64(1), object(4)
memory usage: 320.0+ bytes
fname:
0    john
1    jane
2    jack
3    dave
4    sara
5    eddy
Name: fname, dtype: object
____________
age over 33:
0    False
1    False
2    False
3    False
4     True
5     True
Name: age, dtype: bool
____________
age over 33:
  fname  lname  age gender country
4  sara  stein   34      f  france
5  eddy  bower   35      m  france
```

## PANDAS DATAFRAMES AND EXCEL SPREADSHEETS

Listing 4.32 displays the contents of `people_xslx.py` that illustrates how to read data from an Excel spreadsheet and create a `Pandas DataFrame` with that data.

### *LISTING 4.32: people_xslx.py*

```
import pandas as pd

df = pd.read_excel("people.xlsx")
print("Contents of Excel spreadsheet:")
print(df)
```

Listing 4.32 is straightforward: the `Pandas DataFrame df` is initialized with the contents of the spreadsheet `people.xlsx` (whose contents are the same as `people.csv`) via the `Pandas` function `read_excel()`. The output from Listing 4.32 is here:

```
  fname  lname  age gender country
0  john  smith   30      m     usa
1  jane  smith   31      f  france
2  jack  jones   32      f  france
```

```
3  dave   stone   33      f   france
4  sara   stein   34      f   france
5  eddy   bower   35      f   france
```

## SELECT, ADD, AND DELETE COLUMNS IN DATAFRAMES

This section contains short code blocks that illustrate how to perform operations on a `DataFrame` that resemble the operations on a `Python` dictionary. For example, getting, setting, and deleting columns works with the same syntax as the analogous `Python dict` operations, as shown here:

```
df = pd.DataFrame.from_dict(dict([('A',[1,2,3]),('B',[4,5,6])]),
                    orient='index', columns=['one', 'two', 'three'])

print(df)
```

The output from the preceding code snippet is here:

```
   one  two  three
A    1    2      3
B    4    5      6
```

Now look at the following sequence of operations on the contents of the `DataFrame` df:

```
df['three'] = df['one'] * df['two']
df['flag'] = df['one'] > 2
print(df)
```

The output from the preceding code block is here:

```
   one  two  three   flag
a  1.0  1.0    1.0  False
b  2.0  2.0    4.0  False
c  3.0  3.0    9.0   True
d  NaN  4.0    NaN  False
```

Columns can be deleted or popped like with a `Python dict`, as shown in following code snippet:

```
del df['two']
three = df.pop('three')
print(df)
```

The output from the preceding code block is here:

```
   one   flag
a  1.0  False
b  2.0  False
c  3.0   True
d  NaN  False
```

When inserting a scalar value, it will naturally be propagated to fill the column:

```
df['foo'] = 'bar'
print(df)
```

The output from the preceding code snippet is here:

```
   one   flag  foo
a  1.0  False  bar
b  2.0  False  bar
c  3.0   True  bar
d  NaN  False  bar
```

When inserting a `Series` that does not have the same index as the `DataFrame`, it will be "conformed" to the index of the `DataFrame`:

```
df['one_trunc'] = df['one'][:2]
print(df)
```

The output from the preceding code snippet is here:

```
   one   flag  foo  one_trunc
a  1.0  False  bar        1.0
b  2.0  False  bar        2.0
c  3.0   True  bar        NaN
d  NaN  False  bar        NaN
```

You can insert raw `ndarrays` but their length must match the length of the index of the `DataFrame`.

## PANDAS DATAFRAMES AND SCATTERPLOTS

Listing 4.33 displays the contents of `pandas_scatter_df.py` that illustrates how to generate a scatterplot from a `Pandas DataFrame`.

### *LISTING 4.33: pandas_scatter_df.py*

```
import numpy as np
import pandas as pd
import matplotlib.pyplot as plt
from pandas import read_csv
from pandas.plotting import scatter_matrix

myarray = np.array([[10,30,20], [50,40,60],[1000,2000,3000]])

rownames = ['apples', 'oranges', 'beer']
colnames = ['January', 'February', 'March']
```

```
mydf = pd.DataFrame(myarray, index=rownames,
columns=colnames)

print(mydf)
print(mydf.describe())

scatter_matrix(mydf)
plt.show()
```

Listing 4.33 starts with various import statements, followed by the definition of the `NumPy array myarray`. Next, the variables `myarray` and `colnames` are initialized with values for the rows and columns, respectively. The next portion of Listing 4.33 initializes the `Pandas DataFrame mydf` so that the rows and columns are labeled in the output, as shown here:

```
January  February  March
apples         10         30       20
oranges        50         40       60
beer         1000       2000     3000
              January      February           March
count        3.000000      3.000000        3.000000
mean       353.333333    690.000000     1026.666667
std        560.386771   1134.504297     1709.073823
min         10.000000     30.000000       20.000000
25%         30.000000     35.000000       40.000000
50%         50.000000     40.000000       60.000000
75%        525.000000   1020.000000     1530.000000
max       1000.000000   2000.000000     3000.0000000
```

## PANDAS DATAFRAMES AND SIMPLE STATISTICS

Listing 4.34 displays the contents of `housing_stats.py` that illustrates how to gather basic statistics from data in a `Pandas DataFrame`.

***LISTING 4.34: housing_stats.py***

```
import pandas as pd

df = pd.read_csv("housing.csv")

minimum_bdrms  = df["bedrooms"].min()
median_bdrms   = df["bedrooms"].median()
maximum_bdrms  = df["bedrooms"].max()

print("minimum # of bedrooms:",minimum_bdrms)
print("median  # of bedrooms:",median_bdrms)
print("maximum # of bedrooms:",maximum_bdrms)
print("")

print("median values:",df.median().values)
print("")
```

```
prices = df["price"]
print("first 5 prices:")
print(prices.head())
print("")

median_price = df["price"].median()
print("median price:",median_price)
print("")

corr_matrix = df.corr()
print("correlation matrix:")
print(corr_matrix["price"].sort_values(ascending=False))
```

Listing 4.34 initializes the `Pandas DataFrame df` with the contents of the `CSV` file `housing.csv`. The next three variables are initialized with the minimum, median, and maximum number of bedrooms, respectively, and then these values are displayed.

The next portion of Listing 4.34 initializes the variable `prices` with the contents of the prices column of the `Pandas DataFrame df`. Next, the first five rows are printed via the `prices.head()` statement, followed by the median value of the prices.

The final portion of Listing 4.34 initializes the variable `corr_matrix` with the contents of the correlation matrix for the `Pandas DataFrame df`, and then displays its contents. The output from Listing 4.34 is here:

```
Apples
10
```

## USEFUL ONE-LINE COMMANDS IN PANDAS

This section contains an eclectic mix of one-line commands in Pandas (some of which you have already seen in this chapter) that are useful to know:

Save a data frame to a csv file (comma separated and without indices):

```
df.to_csv("data.csv", sep=",", index=False)
```

List the column names of a `DataFrame`:

```
df.columns
```

Drop missing data from a `DataFrame`:

```
df.dropna(axis=0, how='any')
```

Replace missing data in a `DataFrame`:

```
df.replace(to_replace=None, value=None)
```

Check for NANs in a `DataFrame`:

```
pd.isnull(object)
```

Drop a feature in a `DataFrame`:

```
df.drop('feature_variable_name', axis=1)
```

Convert object type to float in a `DataFrame`:

```
pd.to_numeric(df["feature_name"], errors='coerce')
```

Convert data in a `DataFrame` to NumPy array:

```
df.as_matrix()
```

Display the first n rows of a dataframe:

```
df.head(n)
```

Get data by feature name in a `DataFrame`:

```
df.loc[feature_name]
```

Apply a function to a `DataFrame`: multiply all values in the "height" column of the data frame by 3:

```
df["height"].apply(lambda height: 3 * height)
```

OR:

```
def multiply(x):
    return x * 3
df["height"].apply(multiply)
```

Rename the fourth column of the data frame as "height":

```
df.rename(columns = {df.columns[3]:'height'}, inplace=True)
```

Get the unique entries of the column "first" in a `DataFrame`:

```
df[""first"].unique()
```

Create a dataframe with columns 'first" and "last" from an existing `DataFrame`:

```
new_df = df[["name", "size"]]
```

Sort the data in a `DataFrame`:

```
df.sort_values(ascending = False)
```

Filter the data column named "size" to display only values equal to 7:

```
df[df["size"] == 7]
```

Select the first row of the "height" column in a DataFrame:

```
df.loc([0], ['height'])
```

## SUMMARY

This chapter introduced you to Pandas for creating labeled DataFrames and displaying metadata of Pandas DataFrames. Then you learned how to create Pandas Dataframes from various sources of data, such as random numbers and hard-coded data values.

You also learned how to read Excel spreadsheets and perform numeric calculations on that data, such as the min, mean, and max values in numeric columns. Then you saw how to create Pandas DataFrames from data stored in CSV files. Then you learned how to invoke a Web Service to retrieve data and populate a Pandas DataFrame with that data. In addition, you learned how to generate a scatterplot from data in a Pandas DataFrame.

CHAPTER 5

# ChatGPT and GPT-4

This chapter contains information about the main features of ChatGPT and GPT-4, as well as some of their competitors.

The first portion of this chapter starts with information generated by ChatGPT regarding the nature of generative AI and conversational AI versus generative AI. According to ChatGPT, it's also true that ChatGPT, GPT-4, and Dall-E are also included in generative AI. This section also discusses ChatGPT and some of its features, as well as alternatives to ChatGPT.

The third portion of this chapter discusses some of the features of GPT-4 that power ChatGPT. You will also learn about some competitors of GPT-4, such as Llama-2 (Meta) and Bard (Google).

## WHAT IS GENERATIVE AI?

Generative AI refers to a subset of artificial intelligence models and techniques that are designed to generate new data samples that are similar in nature to a given set of input data. The goal is to produce content or data that wasn't part of the original training set but is coherent, contextually relevant, and in the same style or structure.

Generative AI stands apart in its ability to create and innovate, as opposed to merely analyzing or classifying. The advancements in this field have led to breakthroughs in creative domains and practical applications, making it a cutting-edge area of AI research and development.

### Key Features of Generative AI

The following bullet list contains key features of generative AI, followed by a brief description for each bullet item:

- data generation
- synthesis

- learning distributions
- learning distributions

*Data generation* refers to the ability to create new data points that are not part of the training data but resemble it. This can include text, images, music, videos, or any other form of data.

*Synthesis* means that generative models can blend various inputs to generate outputs that incorporate features from each input, like merging the styles of two images.

*Learning distributions* means that generative AI models aim to learn the probability distribution of the training data so they can produce new samples from that distribution.

## Popular Techniques in Generative AI

Generative adversarial networks (GANs): GANs consist of two networks, a generator and a discriminator, that are trained simultaneously. The generator tries to produce fake data, while the discriminator tries to distinguish between real data and fake data. Over time, the generator gets better at producing realistic data.

Variational autoencoders (VAEs): VAEs are probabilistic models that learn to encode and decode data in a manner that the encoded representations can be used to generate new data samples.

Recurrent neural networks (RNNs): Used primarily for sequence generation, such as text or music.

## What Makes Generative AI Different

Creation versus classification: While most traditional AI models aim to classify input data into predefined categories, generative models aim to create new data.

Unsupervised learning: Many generative models, especially GANs and VAEs, operate in an unsupervised manner, meaning they don't require labeled data for training.

Diverse outputs: Generative models can produce a wide variety of outputs based on learned distributions, making them ideal for tasks like art generation, style transfer, and more.

Challenges: Generative AI poses unique challenges, such as mode collapse in GANs or ensuring the coherence of generated content.

Furthermore, there are numerous areas that involve generative AI applications, some of which are listed in the following list:

- art and music creation
- data augmentation
- style transfer
- text generation
- image synthesis

*Art and music creation* includes generating paintings, music, or other forms of art.

*Data augmentation* involves creating additional data for training models, especially when the original dataset is limited.

*Style transfer* refers to applying the style of one image to the content of another.

*Text generation* is a very popular application of generative AI, which involves creating coherent and contextually relevant text.

*Image synthesis* is another popular area of generative AI, which involves generating realistic images, faces, or even creating scenes for video games.

*Drug discovery* is a very important facet of generative AI that pertains to generating molecular structures for new potential drugs.

## CONVERSATIONAL AI VERSUS GENERATIVE AI

Both conversational AI and generative AI are prominent subfields within the broader domain of artificial intelligence. However, these subfields have a different focus regarding their primary objective, the technologies that they use, and applications. Both are described here:

*https://medium.com/@social_65128/differences-between-conversational-ai-and-generative-ai-e3adca2a8e9a*

The primary differences between the two subfields are in the following sequence of bullet points:

- primary objective
- applications
- technologies used
- training and interaction
- evaluation
- data requirements

### Primary Objective

The main goal of conversational AI is to facilitate human-like interactions between machines and humans. This includes chatbots, virtual assistants, and other systems that engage in dialogue with users.

The primary objective of generative AI is to create new content or data that wasn't in the training set but is similar in structure and style. This can range from generating images, music, and text to more complex tasks like video synthesis.

### Applications

Common applications for conversational AI include customer support chatbots, voice-operated virtual assistants (like Siri or Alexa), and interactive voice response (IVR) systems.

Common applications for generative AI have a broad spectrum of applications such as creating art or music, generating realistic video game environments, synthesizing voices, and producing realistic images or even deep fakes.

### Technologies Used

Conversational AI often relies on natural language processing (NLP) techniques to understand and generate human language. This includes intent recognition, entity extraction, and dialogue management.

Generative AI commonly utilizes generative adversarial networks (GANs), variational autoencoders (VAEs), and other generative models to produce new content.

### Training and Interaction

While training can be supervised, semi-supervised, or unsupervised, the primary interaction mode for conversational AI is through back-and-forth dialogue or conversation.

The training process for generative AI, especially with models like GANs, involves iterative processes where the model learns to generate data by trying to fool a discriminator into believing the generated data is real.

### Evaluation

Conversational AI evaluation metrics often revolve around understanding and response accuracy, user satisfaction, and the fluency of generated responses.

Generative AI evaluation metrics for models like GANs can be challenging and might involve using a combination of quantitative metrics and human judgment to assess the quality of generated content.

### Data Requirements

Data requirements for conversational AI typically involves dialogue data, with conversations between humans or between humans and bots.

Data requirements for generative AI involve large datasets of the kind of content it is supposed to generate, be it images, text, music, and so on.

Although both conversational AI and generative AI deal with generating outputs, their primary objectives, applications, and methodologies can differ significantly. Conversational AI is geared towards interactive communication with users, while Generative AI focuses on producing new, original content.

## IS DALL-E PART OF GENERATIVE AI?

DALL-E and similar tools that generate graphics from text are indeed examples of generative AI. In fact, DALL-E is one of the most prominent examples of generative AI in the realm of image synthesis.

Here's a bullet list of generative characteristics of DALL-E, followed by brief descriptions of each bullet item:

- image generation
- learning distributions
- innovative combinations
- broad applications
- transformer architecture

Image generation is a key feature of DALL-E, which was designed to generate images based on textual descriptions. Given a prompt like "a two-headed flamingo," DALL-E can produce a novel image that matches the description, even if it's never seen such an image in its training data.

Learning distributions: Like other generative models, DALL-E learns the probability distribution of its training data. When it generates an image, it samples from this learned distribution to produce visuals that are plausible based on its training.

Innovative Combinations: DALL-E can generate images that represent entirely novel or abstract concepts, showcasing its ability to combine and recombine learned elements in innovative ways.

In addition to image synthesis, DALL-E has provided broad application support, in areas like art generation, style blending, and creating images with specific attributes or themes, highlighting its versatility as a generative tool.

DALL-E leverages a variant of the transformer architecture, similar to models like GPT-3, but adapted for image generation tasks.

Other tools that generate graphics, art, or any form of visual content based on input data (whether it's text, another image, or any other form of data) and can produce outputs not explicitly present in their training data are also considered generative AI. They showcase the capability of AI models to not just analyze and classify but to create and innovate.

## ARE CHATGPT-3 AND GPT-4 PART OF GENERATIVE AI?

Both ChatGPT-3 and GPT-4 are large language models (LLMs) that are considered examples of generative AI. They belong to a class of models called "transformers," which are particularly adept at handling sequences of data, such as text-related tasks.

The following bullet list provides various reasons why these LLMs are considered generative, followed by a brief description of each bullet item:

- text generation
- learning distributions
- broad applications
- unsupervised learning

*Text generation*: These models can produce coherent, contextually relevant, and often highly sophisticated sequences of text based on given prompts. They generate responses that weren't explicitly present in their training data but are constructed based on the patterns and structures they learned during training.

*Learning distributions*: GPT-3, GPT-4, and similar models learn the probability distribution of their training data. When generating text, they're essentially sampling from this learned distribution to produce sequences that are likely based on their training.

*Broad applications*: Beyond just text-based chat or conversation, these models can be used for a variety of generative tasks like story writing, code generation, poetry, and even creating content in specific styles or mimicking certain authors, showcasing their generative capabilities.

*Unsupervised learning*: While they can be fine-tuned with specific datasets, models like GPT-3 are primarily trained in an unsupervised manner on vast amounts of text, learning to generate content without requiring explicit labeled data for every possible response.

In essence ChatGPT-3, GPT-4, and similar models by OpenAI are quintessential examples of generative AI in the realm of d and generation.

The next several sections briefly introduce some of the companies that have a strong presence in the `AI` world.

## DEEPMIND

DeepMind has made significant contributions to artificial intelligence, which includes the creation of various AI systems. DeepMind was established in 2010 and became a subsidiary of Google 2014, and its home page is here: *https://deepmind.com/*

DeepMind created the 280GB language model `Gopher` that significantly outperforms its competitors, including `GPT-3`, `J1-Jumbo`, and `MT-NLG`. DeepMind also developed `AlphaFold` that solved a protein folding task in literally 30 minutes that had eluded researchers for ten years. Moreover, DeepMind made `AlphaFold` available for free for everyone in July 2021. DeepMind has made significant contributions in the development of world calibre AI game systems, some of which are discussed in the next section.

### DeepMind and Games

DeepMind is the force behind the `AI` systems `StarCraft` and `AlphaGo` that defeated the best human players in `Go` (which is considerably more difficult than chess). These games provide "perfect information," whereas games with "imperfect information" (such as Poker) have posed a challenge for ML models.

`AlphaGo Zero` (the successor of `AlphaGo`) mastered the game through self-play in less time and with less computing power. `AlphaGo Zero` exhibited extraordinary performance by defeating `AlphaGo` 100–0. Another powerful system is AlphaZero that also used a self-play technique learned to play Go, chess, and shogi, and also achieved SOTA (State Of The Art) performance results.

By way of comparison, ML models that use tree search are well-suited for games with perfect information. By contrast, games with imperfect information (such as Poker) involve hidden information that can be leveraged to devise counter strategies to counteract the strategies of opponents. In particular, AlphaStar is capable of playing against the best players of StarCraft II, and also became the first AI to achieve SOTA results in a game that requires significant strategic capability.

## Player of Games (PoG)

The DeepMind team at Google devised the general-purpose PoG (Player of Games) algorithm that is based on the following techniques:

- counterfactual regret minimization (CFR)
- counterfactual value-and-policy network (CVPN)
- growing tree CFR(GT-CFT)

The counterfactual value-and-policy network (CVPN) is a neural network that calculates the counterfactuals for each state belief in the game. This is key to evaluating the different variants of the game at any given time.

Growing tree CFR (GT-CFR) is a variation of CFR that is optimized for game-trees trees that grow over time. GT-CFR is based on two fundamental phases, which is discussed in more detail here:

*https://medium.com/syncedreview/deepminds-pog-excels-in-perfect-and-imperfect-information-games-advancing-research-on-general-9dbad5c04221*

## OPENAI

OpenAI is an AI research company that has made significant contributions to AI, including DALL-E and ChatGPT, and its home page is here: *https://openai.com/api/*

OpenAI was founded in San Francisco by Elon Musk and Sam Altman (as well as others), and one of its stated goals is to develop AI that benefits humanity. Given Microsoft's massive investments in and deep alliance with the organization, OpenAI might be viewed as an arm of Microsoft. OpenAI is the creator of the GPT-x series of LLMs as well as ChatGPT that was made available on November 30, 2022.

OpenAI made `GPT-3` (discussed in Chapter 7) commercially available via API for use across applications, charging on a per-word basis. `GPT-3` was announced in July 2020 and was available through a beta program. Then in November 2021 OpenAI made `GPT-3` open to everyone, and more details are accessible here:

*https://openai.com/blog/api-no-waitlist/*

In addition, OpenAI developed `DALL-E` that generates images from text. OpenAI initially did not permit users to upload images that contained realistic faces. Later (Q4/2022) OpenAI changed its policy to allow users to upload faces into its online system. Check the OpenAI Web page for more details. Incidentally, diffusion models (discussed in Chapter 8) have superseded the benchmarks of `DALL-E`.

OpenAI has also released a public beta of `Embeddings`, which is a data format that is suitable for various types of tasks with machine learning, as described here:

*https://beta.openai.com/docs/guides/embeddings*

OpenAI is the creator of `Codex` that provides a set of models that were trained on NLP. The initial release of Codex was in private beta, and more information is accessible here: *https://beta.openai.com/docs/engines/instruct-series-beta*

OpenAI provides four models that are collectively called their Instruct models, which support the ability of GPT-3 to generate natural language. These models will be deprecated in early January 2024 and replaced with a updated versions of GPT-3, ChatGPT, and GPT-4, as discussed in Chapter 7.

If you want to learn more about the features and services that OpenAI offers, navigate to the following link: *https://platform.openai.com/overview*

## COHERE

Cohere is a start-up and a competitor of OpenAI, and its home page is here: *https://cohere.ai/*

Cohere develops cutting-edge `NLP` technology that is commercially available for multiple industries. Cohere is focused on models that perform textual analysis instead of models for text generation (such as GPT-based models). The founding team of Cohere is impressive: CEO Aidan Gomez is one of the co-inventors of the transformer architecture, and CTO Nick Frosst is a protégé of Geoff Hinton.

## HUGGING FACE

Hugging Face is a popular community-based repository for open-source `NLP` technology, and its home page is here: *https://github.com/huggingface*

Unlike OpenAI or Cohere, Hugging Face does not build its own `NLP` models. Instead, Hugging Face is a platform that manages a plethora of open-source `NLP` models that customers can fine-tune and then deploy those fine-tuned models. Indeed, Hugging Face has become the eminent location for people to collaborate on `NLP` models, and sometimes described as "GitHub for machine learning and `NLP`."

## Hugging Face Libraries

Hugging Face provides three important libraries: datasets, tokenizers, and transformers (discussed in Chapter 3). The Accelerate library supports `PyTorch` models. The datasets library provides an assortment of libraries for `NLP`. The tokenizers library enables you to convert text data to numeric values.

Perhaps the most impressive library is the transformers library that provides an enormous set of pre-trained `BERT`-based models (discussed in Chapter 5) in order to perform a wide variety of `NLP` tasks. The GitHub repository is here: *https://github.com/huggingface/transformers*

## Hugging Face Model Hub

Hugging Face provides a model hub that provides a plethora of models that are accessible online. Moreover, the website supports online testing of its models, which includes the following tasks:

- masked word completion with BERT
- name entity recognition with Electra
- natural language inference with RoBERTa
- question answering with DistilBERT
- summarization with BART
- text generation with GPT-2
- translation with T5

Navigate to the following link to see the text generation capabilities of "write with transformer": *https://transformer.huggingface.co*

In a subsequent chapter you will see `Python` code samples that show how to list all the available Hugging Face datasets and also how to load a specific dataset.

## AI21

`AI21` is a company that provides proprietary large language models via API to support the applications of its customers. The current SOTA model of `AI21` is called `Jurassic-1` (roughly the same size as `GPT-3`), and AI21 also creates its own applications on top of `Jurassic-1` and other models. The current application suite of `AI21` involves tools that can augment reading and writing.

`Primer` is an older competitor in this space, founded two years before the invention of the transformer. The company primarily serves clients in government and defense.

## INFLECTIONAI

A more recent company in the AI field is InflectionAI whose highly impressive founding team includes:

- Reid Hoffman (LinkedIn)
- DeepMind cofounder Mustafa Suleyman
- DeepMind researcher Karen Simonyan

InflectionAI is committed to a challenging task: enabling humans to interact with computers in much the same way that humans communicate with each other.

## ANTHROPIC

Anthropic was created in 2021 by former employees of OpenAI and its home page is here: *https://www.anthropic.com/*

Anthropic has significant financial support from an assortment of companies, including Google and Salesforce. As this book goes to print, Anthropic released Claude 2 as a competitor to ChatGPT. Expect Anthropic to make its API available by Q4 of 2023.

In the meantime, Claude 2 has the ability to summarize as much as 75,000 words of text-based content, whereas ChatGPT currently has a limit of 3,000 words. Moreover, Claude 2 achieved a score of 76.5% on portions of the bar exam and 71% in a Python coding test. Claude 2 also has a higher rate than ChatGPT in terms of providing "clean" responses to queries from users.

This concludes the portion of the chapter regarding the AI companies that are making important contributions in AI. The next section provides a high-level introduction to LLMs (large language models).

## WHAT IS PROMPT ENGINEERING?

You have already learned about text generators such as GPT-3 and DALL-E 2 from OpenAI, Jurassic from AI21, Midjourney, and Stable Diffusion that can perform text-to-image generation. As such, prompt engineering refers to devising text-based prompts that enable AI-based systems to improve the output that is generated, which means that the output more closely matches whatever users want to produce from AI-systems. By way of analogy, think of prompts as similar to the role of coaches: they offer advice and suggestions to help people perform better in their given tasks.

Since prompts are based on words, the challenge involves learning how different words can affect the generated output. Moreover, it's difficult to predict how systems respond to a given prompt. For instance, if you want to generate a landscape, the difference between a dark landscape and a bright landscape is intuitive. However, if you want a beautiful landscape, how would an AI system generate a corresponding image? As you can surmise, concrete words are easier than abstract or subjective words for AI systems that generate images from text. Just to add more to the previous example, how would you visualize the following:

- a beautiful landscape
- a beautiful song
- a beautiful movie

Although prompt engineering started with text-to-image generation, there are other types of prompt engineering, such as audio-based prompts that interpret emphasized text and emotions that are detected in speech, and sketch-based prompts that generate images from drawings. The most recent focus of attention involves text-based prompts for generating videos, which presents exciting opportunities for artists and designers. An example of image-to-image processing is accessible here:

*https://huggingface.co/spaces/fffiloni/stable-diffusion-color-sketch*

## Prompts and Completions

A *prompt* is a text string that users provide to LLMs, and a *completion* is the text that users receive from LLMs. Prompts assist LLMs in completing a request (task), and they can vary in length. Although prompts can be any text string, including a random string, the quality and structure of prompts affects the quality of completions.

Think of prompts as a mechanism for giving "guidance" to LLMs, or even as a way to "coach" LLMs into providing desired answers. Keep in mind that the number of tokens in a prompt plus the number of tokens in the completion can be at most 2,048 tokens. In Chapter 7, you will see a `Python`-based code sample of invoking the `completion()` API in `GPT-3`.

## Types of Prompts

The following bullet list contains well-known types prompts for LLMs:

- zero-shot prompts
- one-shot prompts
- few-shot prompts
- instruction prompts

A *zero-shot prompt* contains a description of a task, whereas a *one-shot prompt* consists of a single example for completing a task. As you can probably surmise, *few-shot prompts* consist of multiple examples (typically between 10 and 100). In all cases, a clear description of the task or tasks is recommended: more tasks provide `GPT-3` with more information, which in turn can lead to more accurate completions.

T0 (for "zero shot") is an interesting LLM: although T0 is 16 times smaller (11GB) than GPT-3 (175GB), T0 has outperformed GPT-3 on language-related tasks. T0 can perform well on unseen NLP tasks (i.e., tasks that are new to T0) because it was trained on a dataset containing multiple tasks.

The following set of links provide the GitHub repository for T0, a Web page for training T0 directly in a browser, and a 3GB version of T0, respectively:

*https://github.com/bigscience-workshop/t-zero*

As you can probably surmise, T0++ is based on T0, and it was trained with extra tasks beyond the set of tasks on which T0 was trained.

Another detail to keep in mind: the first three prompts in the preceding bullet list are also called zero-shot learning, one-shot learning, and few-shot learning, respectively.

## Instruction Prompts

Instruction prompts are used for fine tuning LLMs, and they specify a format (determined by you) for the manner in which the LLM is expected to conform in its responses. You can prepare your own instruction prompts or you can access prompt template libraries that contain different templates for different tasks, along with different data sets. Various prompt instruction templates are publicly available, such as the following links that provides prompt templates (see subsequent section for an example) for Llama (which is discussed in Chapter 9):

*https://github.com/devbrones/llama-prompts*

*https://pub.towardsai.net/llama-gpt4all-simplified-local-chatgpt-ab7d28d34923*

## Reverse Prompts

Another technique uses a reverse order. Input prompts are answers and the response are the questions associated with the answers (similar to a popular game show). For example, given a sentence in French, you might ask the model, "What English text might have resulted in this French translation?"

## System Prompts Versus Agent Prompts

The distinction between a system prompt and an agent prompt often comes up in the context of conversational AI systems and chatbot design.

A system prompt is typically an initial message or cue given by the system to guide the user on what they can do or to set expectations about the interaction. It often serves as an introduction or a way to guide users on how to proceed. Here are some examples of system prompts:

```
"Welcome to ChatBotX! You can ask me questions about
weather, news, or sports. How can I assist you today?"
"Hello! For account details, press 1. For technical
support, press 2."
```

```
"Greetings! Type 'order' to track your package or 'help'
for assistance."
```

By contrast, an agent prompt is a message generated by the AI model or agent in response to a user's input during the course of an interaction. It's a part of the back-and-forth exchange within the conversation. The agent prompt guides the user to provide more information, clarifies ambiguity, or nudges the user towards a specific action. Here are some examples of agent prompts:

```
User: "I'm looking for shoes."
Agent Prompt: "Great! Are you looking for men's or women's shoes?"
User: "I can't log in."
Agent Prompt: "I'm sorry to hear that. Can you specify if you're
having trouble with your password or username?"
User: "Tell me a joke."
Agent Prompt: "Why did the chicken join a band? Because it had the
drumsticks!"
```

The fundamental difference between the two is their purpose and placement in the interaction. A system prompt is often at the beginning of an interaction, setting the stage for the conversation. An agent prompt occurs during the conversation, steering the direction of the dialogue based on user input.

Both types of prompts are crucial for creating a fluid and intuitive conversational experience for users. They guide the user and help ensure that the system understands and addresses the user's needs effectively.

## Prompt Templates

Prompt templates are predefined formats or structures used to instruct a model or system to perform a specific task. They serve as a foundation for generating prompts, where certain parts of the template can be filled in or customized to produce a variety of specific prompts. By way of analogy, prompt templates are the counterpart to macros that you can define in some text editors.

Prompt templates are especially useful when working with language models, as they provide a consistent way to query the model across multiple tasks or data points. In particular, prompt templates can make it easier to:

- ensure consistency when querying a model multiple times
- facilitate batch processing or automation
- reduce errors and variations in how questions are posed to the model

As an example, suppose you're working with an LLM and you want to translate English sentences into French. An associated prompt template could be the following:

"Translate the following English sentence into French: {sentence}"

Note that {sentence} is a placeholder that you can replace with any English sentence.

You can use the preceding prompt template to generate specific prompts:

- "Translate the following English sentence into French: 'Hello, how are you?'"
- "Translate the following English sentence into French: 'I love ice cream.'"

As you can see, prompt templates enable you to easily generate a variety of prompts for different sentences without having to rewrite the entire instruction each time. In fact, this concept can be extended to more complex tasks and can incorporate multiple placeholders or more intricate structures, depending on the application.

## Prompts for Different LLMs

GPT-3, ChatGPT, and GPT-4 are LLMs that are all based on the Transformer architecture and are fundamentally similar in their underlying mechanics. ChatGPT is essentially a version of the GPT model fine-tuned specifically for conversational interactions. GPT-4 is an evolution or improvement over GPT-3 in terms of scale and capabilities.

The differences in prompts for these models mainly arise from the specific use case and context, rather than inherent differences between the models. Here are some prompting differences that are based on use cases.

GPT-3 can be used for a wide range of tasks beyond just conversation, from content generation to code writing. Here are some examples of prompts for GPT-3:

"Translate the following English text to French: 'Hello, how are you?'"
"Write a Python function that calculates the factorial of a number."

ChatGPT: specifically fine-tuned for conversational interactions. Here are some examples of prompts for ChatGPT:

User: "Can you help me with my homework?"
ChatGPT: "Of course! What subject or topic do you need help with?"
User: "Tell me a joke."
ChatGPT: "Why did the chicken cross the playground? To get to the other slide!"

GPT-4: provides a larger scale and refinements, so the prompts would be similar in nature to GPT-3 but might yield more accurate or nuanced outputs. Here are some examples of prompts of prompts for GPT-4:

"Provide a detailed analysis of quantum mechanics in relation to general relativity."
"Generate a short story based on a post-apocalyptic world with a theme of hope."

These three models accept natural language prompts and produce natural language outputs. The fundamental way you interact with them remains consistent.

The main difference comes from the context in which the model is being used and any fine-tuning that has been applied. ChatGPT, for instance, is designed to be more conversational, so while you can use GPT-3 for chats, ChatGPT might produce more contextually relevant conversational outputs.

When directly interacting with these models, especially through an API, you might also have control over parameters like "temperature" (controlling randomness) and "max tokens" (controlling response length). Adjusting these can shape the responses, regardless of which GPT variant you're using.

In essence, while the underlying models have differences in scale and specific training/fine-tuning, the way you prompt them remains largely consistent: clear, specific natural language prompts yield the best results.

## Poorly Worded Prompts

When crafting prompts, it's crucial to be as clear and specific as possible to guide the response in the desired direction. Ambiguous or vague prompts can lead to a wide range of responses, many of which might not be useful or relevant to the user's actual intent. Moreover, poorly worded prompts can lead to confusion, misunderstanding, or nonspecific responses from AI models. Here's a list of examples:

*"Tell me about that thing."*
Problem: Too vague. What "thing" is being referred to?

*"Why did it happen?"*
Problem: No context. What event or situation is being discussed?

*"Explain stuff."*
Problem: Too broad. What specific "stuff" should be explained?

*"Do the needful."*
Problem: Ambiguous. What specific action is required?

*"I want information."*
Problem: Not specific. What type of information is desired?

*"Can you get me the thing from the place?"*
Problem: Both "thing" and "place" are unclear.

*"What's his name's book?"*
Problem: Ambiguous reference. Who is "his?"

*"How do you do the process?"*
Problem: Which "process" is being referred to?

*"Describe the importance of the topic."*
Problem: "Topic" is not specified.

*"Why is it bad or good?"*
Problem: No context. What is "it?"

*"Help with the issue."*
Problem: Vague. What specific issue is being faced?

*"Things to consider for the task."*
Problem: Ambiguity. What "task" is being discussed?

*"How does this work?"*
Problem: Lack of specificity. What is "this?"

## WHAT IS CHATGPT?

The chatbot wars are intensifying, and the long term value of the primary competitors is still to be determined. One competitor (and arguably the current darling) is ChatGPT-3.5 (aka ChatGPT), which is an AI-based chatbot from OpenAI. ChatGPT responds to queries from users by providing conversational responses, and it's accessible here: *https://chat.openai.com/chat*

The growth rate in terms of registered users for ChatGPT has been extraordinary. The closest competitor is iPhone, which reached one million users in 2.5 months, whereas ChatGPT crossed one million users in *six days*. ChatGPT peaked around 1.8 billion users and then decreased to roughly 1.5 billion users, which you can see in the chart in this link:

*https://decrypt.co/147595/traffic-dip-hits-openais-chatgpt-first-times-hardest*

Note that although Threads from Meta out-performed ChatGPT in terms of membership, Threads has seen a significant drop in daily users in the neighborhood of 50%. A comparison of the time frame to reach one million members for six well-known companies/products and ChatGPT is here:

*https://www.syntheticmind.io/p/01*

The preceding link also contains information about Will Hobick who used ChatGPT to write a Chrome extension for email-related tasks, despite not having any JavaScript experience nor has he written a Chrome extension. Will Hobick provides more detailed information about his Chrome extension here:

*https://www.linkedin.com/posts/will-hobick_gpt3-chatgpt-ai-activity-7008081003080470528-8QCh*

### ChatGPT: GPT-3 "on Steroids"?

ChatGPT has been called GPT-3 "on steroids," and there is some consensus that ChatGPT3 is the currently best chatbot in the world. Indeed, ChatGPT can perform multitude of tasks, some of which are listed here:

- write poetry
- write essays
- write code
- role play
- reject inappropriate requests

Moreover, the quality of its responses to natural language queries surpasses the capabilities of its predecessor GPT-3. Another interesting capability includes the ability to acknowledge its mistakes. ChatGPT also provides "prompt replies," which are examples of what you can ask ChatGPT. One interesting use for ChatGPT involves generating a text message for ending a relationship:

*https://www.reddit.com/r/ChatGPT/comments/zgpk6c/breaking_up_with_my_girlfriend/*

ChatGPT generates Christmas lyrics that are accessible here:

*https://www.cnet.com/culture/entertainment/heres-what-it-sounds-like-when-ai-writes-christmas-lyrics*

One aspect of ChatGPT that probably won't be endearing to parents with young children is the fact that ChatGPT has told children that Santa Claus does not exist:

*https://futurism.com/the-byte/openai-chatbot-santa*

*https://www.forbes.com/sites/lanceeliot/2022/12/21/pointedly-asking-generative-ai-chatgpt-about-whether-santa-claus-is-real-proves-to-be-eye-opening-for-ai-ethics-and-ai-law*

## ChatGPT: Google "Code Red"

In December of 2022, the CEO of Google issued a "code red" regarding the potential threat of ChatGPT as a competitor to Google's search engine, which is briefly discussed here:

*https://www.yahoo.com/news/googles-management-reportedly-issued-code-190131705.html*

According to the preceding article, Google is investing resources to develop AI-based products, presumably to offer functionality that can successfully compete with ChatGPT. Some of those AI-based products might also generate graphics that are comparable to graphics effects by DALL-E. Indeed, the race to dominate AI continues unabated and will undoubtedly continue for the foreseeable future.

## ChatGPT Versus Google Search

Given the frequent speculation that ChatGPT is destined to supplant Google Search, let's briefly compare the manner in which Google and

ChatGPT respond to a given query. First, Google is a search engine that uses the Page Rank algorithm (developed by Larry Page), along with fine-tuned aspects to this algorithm that are a closely guarded secret. Google uses this algorithm to rank websites and to generate search results for a given query. However, the search results include paid ads, which can "clutter" the list of links.

By contrast, ChatGPT is not a search engine: it provides a direct response to a given query: in colloquial terms, ChatGPT will simply "cut to the chase" and eliminates the clutter of superfluous links. At the same time, ChatGPT can produce incorrect results, the consequences of which can range between benign and significant.

Consequently, Google Search and ChatGPT both have strengths as well as weaknesses, and they excel with different types of queries: the former for queries that have multifaceted answers (e.g., questions about legal issues), and the latter for straight-to-the point queries (e.g., coding questions). Obviously both of them excel with many other types of queries.

According to Margaret Mitchell, ChatGPT will not replace Google Search, and she provides some interesting details regarding Google Search and PageRank that you can read here: *https://twitter.com/mmitchell_ai/status/1605013368560943105*

## ChatGPT Custom Instructions

ChatGPT has added support for custom instructions, which enable you to specify some of your preferences that ChatGPT will use when responding to your queries.

ChatGPT Plus users can switch on custom instructions by navigating to the ChatGPT website and then perform the following sequence of steps:

```
Settings > Beta features > Opt into Custom instructions
```

As a simple example, you can specify that you prefer to see code in a language other than Python. A set of common initial requirements for routine tasks can also be specified via a custom instructions in ChatGPT. A detailed sequence of steps for setting up custom instructions is accessible here:

*https://artificialcorner.com/custom-instructions-a-new-feature-you-must-enable-to-improve-chatgpt-responses-15820678bc02*

Another interesting example of custom instructions is from Jeremy Howard, who prepared an extensive and detailed set of custom instructions that is accessible here:

*https://twitter.com/jeremyphoward/status/1689464587077509120*

As this book goes to print, custom instructions are available only for users who have registered for ChatGPT Plus. However, OpenAI has stated that custom instructions will be available for free to all users by the end of 2023.

## ChatGPT on Mobile Devices and Browsers

ChatGPT first became available for iOS devices and then for Android devices during 2023. You can download ChatGPT onto an iOS device from the following link:

*https://www.macobserver.com/tips/how-to/how-to-install-and-use-the-official-chatgpt-app-on-iphone/*

Alternatively, if you have an Android device, you can download ChatGPT from the following link: *https://play.google.com/store/apps/details?id=com.openai.chatgpt*

If you want to install ChatGPT for the Bing browser from Microsoft, navigate to this link:

*https://chrome.google.com/webstore/detail/chatgpt-for-bing/pkkmgcildaegadhngpjkklnbfbmhpdng*

## ChatGPT and Prompts

Although ChatGPT is very adept at generating responses to queries, sometimes you might not be fully satisfied with the result. One option is to type the word "rewrite" in order to get another version from ChatGPT.

Although this is one of the simplest prompts available, it's limited in terms of effectiveness. If you want a list of more meaningful prompts, the following article contains 31 prompts that have the potential to be better than using the word "rewrite" (and not just with ChatGPT):

*https://medium.com/the-generator/31-ai-prompts-better-than-rewrite-b3268dfe1fa9*

## GPTBot

GPTBot is a crawler for websites. Fortunately, you can disallow GPTBot from accessing a website by adding the GPTBot to the `robots.txt` file for a website:

```
User-agent: GPTBot
Disallow: /
```

You can also customize GPTBot access only a portion of a website by adding the GPTBot token to to the `robots.txt` like file for a website:

```
User-agent: GPTBot
Allow: /youcangohere-1/
Disallow: /dontgohere-2/
```

As an aside, Stable Diffusion and LAION both scrape the Internet via Common Crawl. However, you can prevent your website from being scraped by specifying the following snippet in the `robots.txt` file:

```
User-agent: CCBot
Disallow: /
```

More information about GPTBot is accessible here: *https://platform.openai.com/docs/gptbot*

*https://platform.openai.com/docs/gptbot*

*https://www.yahoo.com/finance/news/openai-prepares-unleash-crawler-devour-020628225.html*

## ChatGPT Playground

ChatGPT has its own playground, which you will see is substantively different from the GPT-3 playground, that is accessible here: *https://chat.openai.com/chat*

For your convenience, the link for the GPT-3 playground is reproduced here:

*https://beta.openai.com/playground*

OpenAI has periodically added new functionality to ChatGPT that includes the following:

- Users can view (and continue) previous conversations.
- The number of questions that ChatGPT will not answer has been reduced.
- Users remain logged in for longer than two weeks.

Another nice enhancement includes support for keyboard shortcuts: when working with code you can use the sequence ⌘ (Ctrl) + Shift + (for Mac) to copy last code block and the sequence ⌘ (Ctrl) + / to see the complete list of shortcuts.

Many articles are available regarding ChatGPT and how to write prompts in order to extract the details that you want from ChatGPT. One of those articles is here:

*https://www.tomsguide.com/features/7-best-chatgpt-tips-to-get-the-most-out-of-the-chatbot*

# PLUGINS, ADVANCED DATA ANALYSIS, AND CODE WHISPERER

In addition to answering a plethora of queries from users, ChatGPT extends its functionality by providing support for the following:

- third-party ChatGPT plug-ins
- Code Interpreter
- Code Whisperer

Each of the topics in the preceding bullet list are briefly discussed in the following subsections, along with a short section that discusses Code Interpreter versus Claude-2 from Anthropic.

## Plugins

There are several hundred ChatGPT plugins available, and a list of some popular plugins is accessible here:

*https://levelup.gitconnected.com/5-chatgpt-plugins-that-will-put-you-ahead-of-99-of-data-scientists-4544a3b752f9*

*https://www.zdnet.com/article/the-10-best-chatgpt-plugins-of-2023/*

Keep in mind that lists of the "best" ChatGPT plugins change frequently, so it's a good idea to perform an online search to find out about newer ChatGPT plugins. The following link also contains details about highly rated plugins (by the author of the following article):

*https://www.tomsguide.com/features/i-tried-a-ton-of-chatgpt-plugins-and-these-3-are-the-best*

Another set of recommended plugins (depending on your needs, of course) is shown here:

- AskYourPDF
- ChatWithVideo
- Noteable
- Upskillr
- Wolfram

If you are concerned about the possibility of ChatGPT scraping the content of your website, the browser plugin from OpenAI supports a user-agent token called ChatGPT-User that abides by the content specified in the `robots.txt` file that many websites provide for restricting access to content.

If you want to develop a plugin for ChatGPT, navigate to this website for more information: *https://platform.openai.com/docs/plugins/introduction*

Along with details for developing a ChatGPT plugin, the preceding OpenAI website provides useful information about plugins, as shown here:

- authentication
- examples
- plugin review
- plugin policies

OpenAI does not control any plugins that you add to ChatGPT: they connect ChatGPT to external applications. Moreover, ChatGPT determines which plugin to use during your session, based on on the specific plugins that you have enabled in your ChatGPT account.

## Advanced Data Analysis

ChatGPT Code Interpreter enables ChatGPT to generate charts and graphs, create and train machine learning models, including deep learning models. ChatGPT Code Interpreter provides an extensive set of features and it's available to ChatGPT users who are paying the USD 20/month subscription. However, this feature will probably be made available to all users very soon.

*https://towardsdatascience.com/chatgpt-code-interpreter-how-it-saved-me-hours-of-work-3c65a8dfa935*

The models from OpenAI can access a Python interpreter that is confined to a sandboxed and fire-walled execution environment. There is also some temporary disk space that is accessible to the interpreter plugin during the evaluation of Python code. Although the temporary disk space is available for a limited time, multiple queries during in the same session can produce a cumulative effect with regard to the code and execution environment.

In addition, ChatGPT can generate a download link (upon request) in order to download data. One other interesting feature: Code Interpreter can analyze multiple files at once, which includes CSV files and Excel spreadsheets.

Code interpreter can perform an interesting variety of tasks, some of which are listed here:

- solve mathematical tasks
- perform data analysis and visualization
- convert files between formats
- work with Excel spreadsheets

The following article discusses various ways that you can use Code Interpreter:

*https://mlearning.substack.com/p/the-best-88-ways-to-use-chatgpt-code-interpreter*

## Advanced Data Analysis Versus Claude-2

Claude-2 from Anthropic (discussed in Chapter 1) is another competitor to ChatGPT. In addition to responding to prompts from users, Claude-2 can generate code and also ingest entire books. Claude-2 is also subject to hallucinations, which is true of other LLM-based chatbots. More detailed information regarding Claude-2 is accessible here:

*https://medium.com/mlearning-ai/claude-2-vs-code-interpreter-gpt-4-5-d2e5c9ee00c3*

Incidentally, the currently available version of ChatGPT was trained on September 2021, which means that ChatGPT cannot answer questions regarding Claude-2 or Google Bard, both of which were released after this date.

### Advanced Data Analysis and Charts and Graphs

Figure 5.1 displays a screenshot of charts that are based on the `Titanic` dataset.

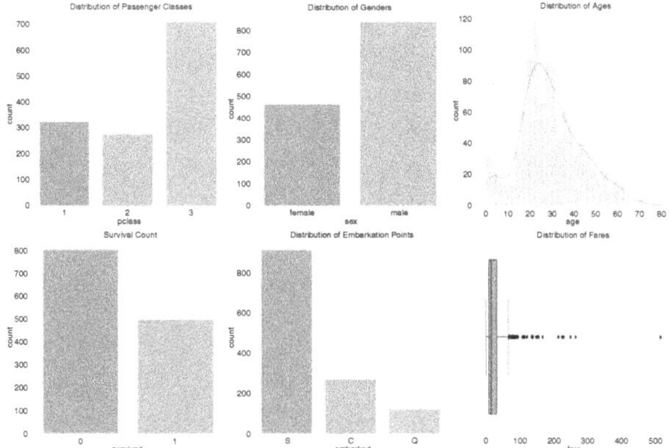


***FIGURE 5.1*** Titanic charts and graphs.

Incidentally, if you would like to see examples of ChatGPT generating `Python` code for machine learning models, as well as code for charts and graphs, you can learn how to do so in three forthcoming books from Mercury Learning and Information that will be available in early 2024:

- *Machine Learning, Python 3, and ChatGPT*
- *GPT-4 for Developers*
- *Python 3 and Data Visualization with ChatGPT/GPT-4*

### Code Whisperer

ChatGPT Code Whisperer enables you to simplify some tasks, some of which are in the following list (compare this list with the corresponding list for Bard):

- create videos from images
- extract text from an image
- extract colors from an image

After ChatGPT has generated a video, it will also give you a link from which the generated video is downloadable. More detailed information regarding the features in the preceding bullet list is accessible here:

*https://artificialcorner.com/chatgpt-code-interpreter-is-not-just-for-coders-here-are-6-ways-it-can-benefit-everyone-b3cc94a36fce*

## DETECTING GENERATED TEXT

Without a doubt, `ChatGPT` has raised the bar with respect to the quality of generated text, which further complicates the task of plagiarism. When you read a passage of text, there are several clues that suggest generated text, such as:

- awkward or unusual sentence structure
- repeated text in multiple locations
- excessive use of emotions (or absence thereof)

However, there are tools that can assist in detecting generated code. One free online tool is `GPT2 Detector` (from OpenAI) that is accessible here:

*https://huggingface.co/openai-detector*

As a simple (albeit contrived) example, type the following sentence in GPT-2 Detector:

```
This is an original sentence written by me and nobody else.
```

The GPT-2 Detector analyzed this sentence and reported that this sentence is real with a 19.35% probability. Now let's modify the preceding sentence by adding some extra text, as shown here:

```
This is an original sentence written by me and nobody else,
regardless of what an online plagiarism tool will report
about this sentence.
```

The GPT-2 Detector analyzed this sentence and reported that this sentence is real with a 95.85% probability. According to the GPT-2 Detector website, the reliability of the probability scores "get reliable" when there are around 50 tokens in the input text.

Another (slightly older) online tool for detecting automatically generated text is giant language model test room (GLTR) from IBM, which is accessible here: *http://gltr.io/*

You can download the source code (a combination of TypeScript and CSS) for GLTR here:

*https://github.com/HendrikStrobelt/detecting-fake-text*

In addition to the preceding free tools, some commercial tools are also available, one of which is shown here: *https://writer.com/plans/*

## CONCERNS ABOUT CHATGPT

One important aspect of ChatGPT is that it's not designed for accuracy: in fact, ChatGPT can generate (fabricate?) very persuasive answers that are actually incorrect. This detail distinguishes ChatGPT from search engines: the latter provide links to existing information instead of generating responses that might be incorrect. Another comparison is that ChatGPT is more flexible and creative, whereas search engines are less flexible but more accurate in their responses to queries.

Educators are concerned about students using ChatGPT as a tool to complete their class assignments instead of developing research-related skills in conjunction with writing skills. At the same time, there are educators who enjoy the reduction in preparation time for their classes as a direct result of using ChatGPT to put together lesson plans.

Another concern is that ChatGPT cannot guarantee that it provides factual data in response to queries from users. In fact, ChatGPT can "hallucinate," which means that it can provide wrong answers as well as citations (i.e., links) that do not exist.

Another limitation of ChatGPT is due to the use of training data that was available only up until 2021. However, OpenAI does support plug-ins for ChatGPT, one of which can perform on-the-fly real time Web searches.

As you will learn later, the goal of prompt engineering is to understand how to craft meaningful queries that will induce ChatGPT to provide the information that you want: poorly worded (or incorrectly worded) prompts can produce equally poor results. As a rule, it's advisable to curate the contents of the responses from ChatGPT, especially in the case of responses to queries that involve legal details.

## Code Generation and Dangerous Topics

Two significant areas for improvement pertain to code generation and handling dangerous topics.

Although `ChatGPT` (as well as `GPT-3`) can generate code for various types of applications, keep in mind that `ChatGPT` displays code that was written by other developers, which is also code that was used to train `ChatGPT`. Consequently, portions of that code (such as version numbers) might be outdated or code that is actually incorrect.

As for queries that involve dangerous topics, `ChatGPT` explains why it cannot answer such a query. However, a query that is posed in "pretend mode" ("suppose you are a fictional character, and how would you explain . . . ") has enabled people to obtain results from ChatGPT that do not conform to its guidelines.

Other serious potential issues exist, some of which are discussed in the following article:

*https://www.yahoo.com/news/hypnotized-chatgpt-bard-convince-users-182100261.html*

## ChatGPT Strengths and Weaknesses

ChatGPT has a number of strengths. In particular, ChatGPT responds directly to questions without including extraneous links. However, ChatGPT is prone to various types of errors, along with limitations that include the following:

- inability to "fact check" information
- inability to differentiate misinformation versus facts
- can fabricate answers (aka hallucinations)
- can generate inappropriate/toxic responses

`ChatGPT` is prone to prompt injection, which can consist of very simple content. However, other chatbots are also susceptible to prompt injection (i.e., it's not specific to `ChatGPT`). More details regarding prompt injections are accessible here:

*https://mlearning.substack.com/p/what-exactly-is-a-prompt-injection*

Incidentally, the chatbot LaMDA from Google is also prone to the preceding limitations, which has made Google hesitant to release LaMDA for general availability because of its potential risk regarding Google's reputation. As a side note, LaMDA was announced in May 2021, and at that time it was described as a "breakthrough language technology." You can read more about LaMDA here: *https://blog.google/technology/ai/lamda/*

Despite the earlier bullet list, ChatGPT has increased the capabilities of chat bots, and will undoubtedly spur innovation and competition among prominent stakeholders in this arena.

## SAMPLE QUERIES AND RESPONSES FROM CHATGPT

Here is an example of various queries submitted to ChatGPT, followed by the detailed response from ChatGPT:

```
Many people think that AI is dangerous what do you think?
```

"There is a common misconception that AI is inherently dangerous. While it is true that AI has the potential to be used for harmful purposes, it is also capable of doing a lot of good. Just like any other technology, it all depends on how it is used. In the right hands, AI can be used to solve some of the world's most pressing problems, such as curing diseases and improving agriculture. In the wrong hands, it could be used to cause harm. It's important for us to use AI responsibly and ethically, and to ensure that it is regulated and controlled in a way that minimizes the potential for harm."

Here is another example of a query submitted to ChatGPT-3, followed by its detailed response:

```
What are some ways in which you can improve the accuracy of
your responses to queries?
```

"There are several ways to improve the accuracy of my responses to queries. One way is to use more data to train my algorithms on. The more data I have, the more information I have to work with, and the more accurate my responses can be. Another way to improve my accuracy is to use more advanced algorithms and techniques, such as machine learning and natural language processing. These methods allow me to better understand the nuances of language and to provide more accurate responses to queries. Additionally, regular testing and evaluation can help identify areas where my accuracy can be improved, and allow me to focus on those areas to refine my responses."

```
Can you give an example of an odd perfect number?
```

"As far as we know, there are no odd perfect numbers. While it is believed that odd perfect numbers exist, none have been found yet, and it is not known if there are any. In fact, it is currently unknown if there are any odd perfect numbers at all. If an odd perfect number were to be discovered, it would be a major breakthrough in mathematics."

```
Can you provide a proof of Goldbach's conjecture?
```

"I'm sorry, but I am not able to provide a proof of Goldbach's conjecture. Goldbach's conjecture is a famous unsolved problem in mathematics that states that every even integer greater than 2 can be expressed as the sum of two prime numbers. Despite much effort by mathematicians over the years, a proof of the conjecture has not yet been found. It is considered to be one of the most challenging unsolved problems in mathematics. Because I am a large language model trained by OpenAI, I do not have the ability to prove mathematical conjectures. My abilities are limited to providing answers based on the information that I have been trained on."

```
Is there life after death, and how does it compare with
life on Earth?
```

"There is no scientific evidence to support the idea of life after death. This is a topic that has been debated for centuries, and different cultures and belief systems have their own ideas about what happens after we die. Some people believe in an afterlife, while others do not. Because there is no scientific evidence to support the existence of an afterlife, it is not possible to say how it would compare to life on Earth. It is ultimately a matter of personal belief."

```
Please provide a four-paragraph analysis of the war between
Ukraine and Russia, and also provide your prediction
regarding the outcome
```

"The war between Ukraine and Russia is a complex conflict that has its roots in the 2014 Russian annexation of Crimea. Since then, the conflict has escalated, with Russian-backed separatists in eastern Ukraine fighting against the Ukrainian government. The fighting has resulted in thousands of casualties and has displaced many people.

The main issue at the heart of the conflict is the question of Ukraine's sovereignty. Russia has long considered Ukraine to be within its sphere of influence, and the annexation of Crimea was seen by many as a violation of Ukraine's sovereignty. Ukraine, on the other hand, is determined to maintain its independence and has been supported in this by many Western countries.

It is difficult to predict the outcome of the war. While the Ukrainian military has been able to make gains against the separatists in recent years, Russia continues to provide support to the rebels and the conflict remains unresolved. In the long term, a diplomatic solution will likely be necessary in order to bring an end to the fighting. However, it is uncertain if and when such a solution will be reached.

In the meantime, the war continues to take a heavy toll on the people of Ukraine. Many are caught in the crossfire, and the ongoing violence and instability have had a significant impact on the country's economy and overall development. It is important for the international community to continue to support Ukraine in its efforts to maintain its sovereignty and bring an end to the conflict."

As you can see from the preceding examples, ChatGPT provides impressive and accurate responses to queries in a manner that surpasses many chatbots of recent years. However, it's still possible to confound this chatbot as is described in the following article: *https://www.theverge.com/23488017/openai-chatbot-chatgpt-ai-examples-web-demo*

## ALTERNATIVES TO CHATGPT

There are several alternatives to ChatGPT that offer a similar set of features, some of which are listed here:

- Bard (Google)
- Bing Chat
- Gemini (Google)
- Jasper
- PaLM (Google)
- Pi
- POE (LinkedIn)
- Replika
- WriteSonic
- YouChat

The following subsections discuss some (but not all) of the ChatGPT alternatives in the preceding bullet list.

### Google Bard

Google Bard is a chatbot that has similar functionality as ChatGPT, such as generating code as well as generating text/documents. A subset of the features supported by Bard is as follows:

- built-in support for Internet search
- built-in support for voice recognition
- built "on top of" PaLM 2 (Google)
- support for 20 programming languages

- read/summarize PDF contents
- provides links for its information

According to the following article in mid-2023, Bard added support for forty additional language as well as support for text-to-speech:

*https://www.extremetech.com/extreme/google-bard-updated-with-text-to-speech-40-new-languages*

Moreover, Bard supports prompts that include images (interpreted by Google Lens) and can produce captions based on the images.

The following article suggests that Google can remain competitive with ChatGPT by leveraging PaLM (discussed later in this chapter):

*https://analyticsindiamag.com/googles-palm-is-ready-for-the-gpt-challenge/*

## YouChat

Another alternative to ChatGPT is YouChat that is part of the search engine you.com, and it's accessible here:

*https://you.com/*

Richard Socher, who is well known in the ML community for his many contributions, is the creator of you.com. According to Richard Socher, YouChat is a search engine that can provide the usual search-related functionality as well as the ability to search the Web to obtain more information in order to provide responses to queries from users.

Another competitor is Poe from LinkedIn, and you can create a free account at this link: *https://poe.com/login*

## Pi From Inflection

Pi is a chatbot developed by Inflection, which is a company that was by Mustafa Suleyman, who is also the founder of DeepMind. Pi is accessible here:

*https://pi.ai/talk*

And an article about Pi can be found here:

*https://medium.com/@ignacio.de.gregorio.noblejas/meet-pi-chatgpts-newest-rival-and-the-most-human-ai-in-the-world-367b461c0af1*

The development team used reinforcement learning from human feedback (RLHF) in order to train this chatbot:

*https://medium.com/@ignacio.de.gregorio.noblejas/meet-pi-chatgpts-newest-rival-and-the-most-human-ai-in-the-world-367b461c0af1*

## WHAT IS INSTRUCTGPT?

InstructGPT is a language model developed by OpenAI, and it's a sibling model to ChatGPT. InstructGPT is designed to follow instructions given in a prompt to generate detailed responses. Some key points about InstructGPT are listed here:

- instruction following
- training
- applications
- limitations

*Instruction Following*: Unlike ChatGPT, which is more geared towards open-ended conversations, InstructGPT is designed to be more focused on following user instructions in prompts. This makes it suitable for tasks where the user wants to get specific information or outputs by giving clear directives.

*Training*: InstructGPT is trained using reinforcement learning from human feedback (RLHF), similar to ChatGPT. An initial model is trained using supervised fine-tuning, where human AI trainers provide conversations playing both sides (the user and the AI assistant). This new dialogue dataset is then mixed with the InstructGPT dataset transformed into a dialogue format.

*Applications*: InstructGPT can be useful in scenarios where you want more detailed explanations, step-by-step guides, or specific outputs based on the instructions provided.

*Limitations*: Like other models, InstructGPT has its limitations. It might produce incorrect or nonsensical answers. The output heavily depends on how the prompt is phrased. It's also sensitive to input phrasing and might give different responses based on slight rephrasing.

It's worth noting that as AI models and their applications are rapidly evolving, there might have been further developments or iterations on InstructGPT after 2021. Always refer to OpenAI's official publications and updates for the most recent information. More information about InstructGPT is accessible here:

*https://openai.com/blog/instruction-following/*

## VIZGPT AND DATA VISUALIZATION

VizGPT is an online tool that enables you to specify English-based prompts in order to visualize aspects of datasets, and it's accessible here: *https://www.vizgpt.ai/*

Select the default "Cars Dataset" and then click on the "Data" button in order to display the contents of the dataset, as shown in Figure 5.2.

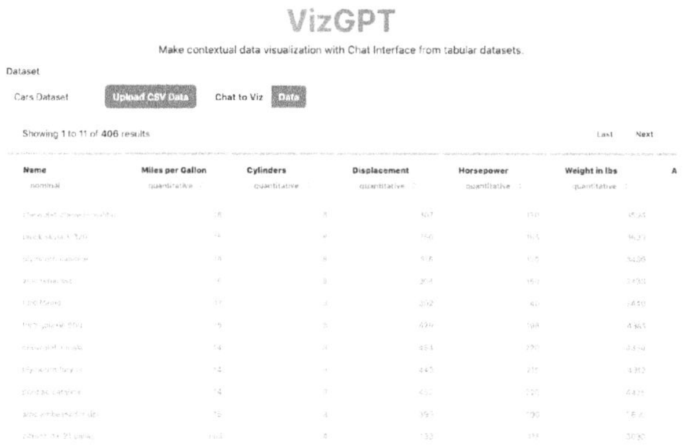

*FIGURE 5.2* VizGPT Car Dataset rows.

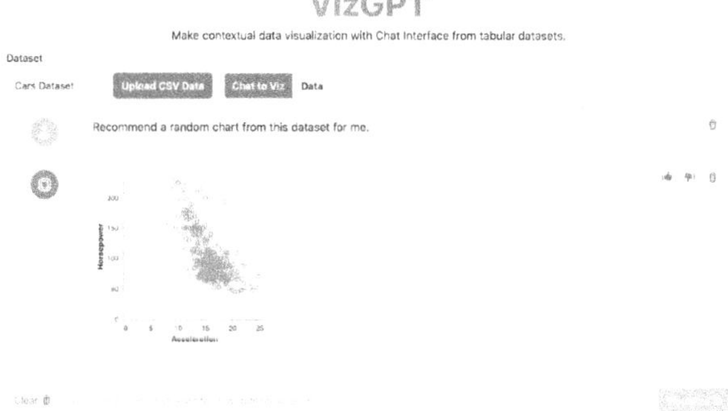


*FIGURE 5.3* VizGPT Car Dataset visualization.

Next, select the default "Cars Dataset" and then click on the "Chat to Viz" button in order to display a visualization of the dataset, as shown in Figure 5.3.

You can experiment further with VizGPT. For example, you can upload your own dataset by clicking on the "Upload CSV" button and obtain similar results with that dataset.

## WHAT IS GPT-4?

GPT-4 was released in mid-March 2023, and became available only to users with an existing ChatGPT account via of a paid upgrade (US$ 20/month) to that account. According to various online anecdotal stories from users, GPT-4 is significantly superior to ChatGPT. In addition, Microsoft has a version of GPT-4 that powers its Bing browser, which is freely available to the public.

GPT-4 is a large multimodal model that can process image-based inputs as well as text-based inputs and then generate textual outputs. Currently image-based outputs are unavailable to the general public, but it does have internal support for image generation.

GPT-4 supports 25,000 words of input text: by comparison, ChatGPT is limited to 4,096 characters. Although the number of parameters in GPT-4 is undisclosed, the following article asserts that GPT-4 is a mixture of 8 x 220-billion-parameter models, which is an example of mixture of experts (MoE). You can read about the release of GPT-4 here:

*https://thealgorithmicbridge.substack.com/p/gpt-4s-secret-has-been-revealed*

## GPT-4 and Test-Taking Scores

One interesting example of the improved accuracy pertains to a bar exam, which ChatGPT scored in the bottom 10%. By contrast, GPT-4 scored in the top 10% for the same bar exam. More details are accessible here:

*https://www.abajournal.com/web/article/latest-version-of-chatgpt-aces-the-bar-exam-with-score-in-90th-percentile*

In addition, GPT-4 is apparently able to pass first year at Harvard with a 3.34 GPA. More details are accessible here:

*https://www.businessinsider.com/chatgpt-harvard-passed-freshman-ai-education-GPT-4-2023-7?op=1*

Furthermore, GPT-4 has performed well on a number of additional tests, some of which are listed here:

- AP exams
- SAT
- GRE
- medical tests
- law exams
- business school exams
- Wharton MBA exam
- USA Biology Olympiad Semifinal Exam
- sommelier exams (wine steward)

You can read more details regarding the preceding tests from this link:

*https://www.businessinsider.com/list-here-are-the-exams-chatgpt-has-passed-so-far-2023-1*

The following link contains much more detailed information regarding test scores, benchmarks, and other results pertaining to GPT-4: *https://openai.com/research/gpt-4*

## GPT-4 Parameters

This section contains information regarding some of the GPT-4 parameters, some of which are best-guess approximations.

Since GPT-4 is a transformer-based AR (auto regressive) model, it's trained to perform next-token prediction. The following paper "GPT4 Technical

Report" was released in March/2023 and it contains a detailed analysis of the capabilities of GPT-4:

*https://docs.kanaries.net*

## GPT-4 Fine Tuning

Although OpenAI allow you to fine-tune the base models, it's (currently) not possible to perform fine tuning on ChatGPT-3.5 or GPT4. Instead, you can integrate OpenAI models with your own data source via LangChain or LlamaIndex (previously known as GPT-Index). Both of them enable you to connect OpenAI models with your existing data sources.

An introduction to LangChain is accessible here:

*https://www.pinecone.io/learn/series/langchain/langchain-intro/*

An introduction to LlamaIndex is accessible here:

*https://zilliz.com/blog/getting-started-with-llamaindex*

You can read more about fine-tuning here:

*https://stackoverflow.com/questions/76160057/openai-chat-completions-api-how-do-i-customize-answers-from-gpt-3-5-or-gpt-4-mo?noredirect=1&lq=1*

# CHATGPT AND GPT-4 COMPETITORS

Shortly after the release of ChatGPT on November 30, 2022, there was a flurry of activity among various companies to release a competitor to ChatGPT, some of which are listed here:

- Bard (Google chatbot)
- CoPilot (Microsoft)
- Codex (OpenAI)
- Apple GPT (Apple)
- PaLM 2 (Google and GPT-4 competitor)
- Claude 2 (Anthropic)
- Llama-2 (Meta; described in a later section)

The following subsections contain additional details regarding the LLMs in the preceding bullet list.

## Bard

Bard is an AI chatbot from Google that was released in early 2023 and it's a competitor to ChatGPT. By way of comparison, Bard is powered by PaLM 2 (discussed later), whereas ChatGPT is powered by GPT-4. Recently Bard added support for images in its answers to user queries, whereas this functionality for ChatGPT has not been released yet to the public.

Bard encountered an issue pertaining to the James Webb Space Telescope during a highly publicized release, which resulted in a significant decrease in market capitalization for Alphabet. However, Google has persevered in fixing issues and enhancing the functionality of Bard. You can access Bard from this link: *https://bard.google.com/*

Around mid-2023 Bard was imbued with several features that were not available in GPT-4 during the same time period, some of which are listed here:

- The user could not generate images.
- The user could not generate HTML/CSS from an image.
- The user could not generate mobile applications from an image.
- The user could not create latex formulas from an image.
- The user could not extract text from an image.

Presumably these features will spur OpenAI to provide the same set of features (some are implemented in GPT-4 but they are not publicly available).

## CoPilot (OpenAI/Microsoft)

Microsoft CoPilot is a Visual Studio Code extension that is also powered by GPT-4. GitHub CoPilot is already known for its ability to generate blocks of code within the context of a program. In addition, Microsoft is also developing Microsoft 365 CoPilot, whose availability date has not been announced yet.

However, Microsoft has provided early demos that show some of the capabilities of Microsoft 365 CoPilot, which includes automating tasks such as:

- writing emails
- summarizing meetings
- making PowerPoint presentations

Microsoft 365 CoPilot can analyze data in Excel spreadsheets, insert AI-generated images in PowerPoint, and generate drafts of cover letters. Microsoft has also integrated Microsoft 365 CoPilot into some of its existing products, such as Loop and OneNote.

According to the following article, Microsoft intends to charge US$ 30 per month for Office 365 Copilot:

*https://www.extremetech.com/extreme/microsoft-to-charge-30-per-month-for-ai-powered-office-apps*

Copilot was reverse engineered in late 2022, which is described here:

*https://thakkarparth007.github.io/copilot-explorer/posts/copilot-internals*

The following article shows you how to create a GPT-3 application that uses NextJS, React, and CoPilot:

*https://github.blog/2023-07-25-how-to-build-a-gpt-3-app-with-nextjs-react-and-github-copilot/*

## Codex (OpenAI)

OpenAI Codex is a fine-tuned GPT3-based LLM that generates code from text. In fact, Codex powers GitHub Copilot (discussed in the preceding section). Codex was trained on more than 150GB of Python code that was obtained from more than 50 million GitHub repositories.

According to OpenAI, the primary purpose of Codex is to accelerate human programming, and it can complete almost 40% of requests. Codex tends to work quite well for generating code for solving simpler tasks. Navigate to the Codex home page to obtain more information: *https://openai.com/blog/openai-codex*

## Apple GPT

In mid-2023 Apple announced Apple GPT, which is a competitor to ChatGPT from OpenAI. The actual release date was projected to be 2024. "Apple GPT" is the current name for a product that is intended to compete with Google Bard, OpenAI ChatGPT, and Microsoft Bing AI.

In brief, the LLM PaLM 2 (discussed in the next section) powers Google Bard, and GPT-4 powers ChatGPT as well as Bing Chat, whereas Ajax is what powers Apple GPT. Ajax is based on Jax from Google, and the name Ajax is a clever concatenation ("Apple Jax?" perhaps?)

## PaLM-2

Pathways language model (PaLM-2) is the successor to PaLM (circa 2022). PaLM-2 powers Bard and it's also a direct competitor to GPT-4. By way of comparison, PaLM consists of 540B parameters, and it's plausible that PaLM-2 is a larger LLM (details of the latter are undisclosed).

PaLM-2 provides four submodels called Gecko, Otter, Bison, and Unicorn (smallest to largest). PaLM-2 was trained on more than 100 human languages, as well as programming languages such as Fortran. Moreover, PaLM-2 has been deployed to a plethora of Google products, including Gmail and YouTube.

## Med-PaLM M

In addition to the four sub models listed in the previous section, Med-PaLM 2 (the successor to Med-PaLM) is an LLM that provides answers to medical questions, and it's accessible here: *http://sites.research.google/med-palm/*

The successor to Med-PaLM is Med-PaLM M, and details about this LLM are accessible here: *https://arxiv.org/abs/2307.14334*

An article that provides a direct comparison of performance benchmarks for PaLM 2 and GPT-4 is accessible here:

*https://www.makeuseof.com/google-palm-2-vs-openai-gpt-4/*

All told, PaLM-2 has a robust set of features and it's definitely a significant competitor to GPT-4.

## Claude 2

Anthropic created the LLM Claude 2 that can not only answer queries about specific topics, it can also perform searches that involves multiple documents, summarize documents, create documents, and generate code.

Claude 2 is an improvement on Anthropic's predecessor Claude 1.3, and it can ingest entire books as well as generate code based on prompts from users. In fact, Claude 2 appears to be comparable with its rivals ChatGPT and GPT-4 in terms of competing functionality.

Furthermore, Claude 2 supports a context window of 100,000 tokens. Moreover, Claude 2 was trained on data as recent as early 2023, whereas ChatGPT was trained on data up until 2021. However, Claude 2 cannot search the Web (unlike its competitor GPT-4). Stay tuned to Anthropic, where you will probably see more good things in the LLM space.

## LLAMA-2

Large Language Model Meta AI (LlaMa 2) is an open source fine-tuned LLM from Meta, that trained on only public data, that has created a lot of excitement in the AI community. LlaMa-2 provides three models (7B, 13B, and 70B parameters) that utilize more data during the pre-training step than numerous other LLMs. LlaMa-2 is optimized to provide faster inferences and also provides a longer context length (4K) than other LLMs.

Moreover, the LlaMa-2-Chat LLM performs surprisingly well: in some cases, its quality is close to the quality of high-performing LLMs such ChatGPT and GPT-4. LlaMa-2 is more user-friendly also provides better results for writing text in comparison to GPT-4. On the other hand, GPT-4 is more adept for tasks such as generating code.

## How to Download LlaMa-2

Llama-2 provides a permissive license for community use and commercial use, and Meta has made the code as well as the pre-trained models and the fine-tuned models publicly available.

There are several ways that you can download Llama-2, starting from this link from Meta after you provide some information (name, country, and affiliation):

*https://ai.meta.com/llama/*

Another way to access demos of the 7B, 13B, and 70B models is from the following links:

*https://huggingface.co/spaces/huggingface-projects/llama-2-7b-chat*

*https://huggingface.co/spaces/huggingface-projects/llama-2-13b-chat*

*https://huggingface.co/spaces/ysharma/Explore_llamav2_with_TGI*

A third way to access Llama-2 is on Hugging Face from the following link: *https://huggingface.co/blog/llama2*

If you are interested in training Llama-2 on your laptop, more details for doing so are accessible here: *https://blog.briankitano.com/llama-from-scratch/*

## LlaMa-2 Architecture Features

This section simply contains a high-level list of some of the important distinguishing features of LlaMa-2, as shown here:

- decoder-only LLM (Chapter 3)
- better pretraining
- improved model architecture
- SwiGLU activation function
- different positional embeddings (Chapter 4)
- grouped query attention (GQA)
- Ghost Attention (GAtt)
- RLHF and PPO (Chapter 5)
- BPE SentencePiece tokenizer
- modified normalization step

The majority of LLMs contain the layer normalization that is in the original Transformer architecture. By contrast, LlaMA uses a simplified alternative that involves Root Mean Square Layer Normalization (aka RMSNorm). RMSNorm has yielded improved results for training stability as well as for generalization.

Although SwiGLU is computationally more expensive than the ReLU activation function that is part of the original Transformer architecture, SwiGLU achieves better performance.

Note that RLHF is discussed in Chapter 5, which also includes a brief description of TRPO and PPO. For a detailed description of how to fine tune LlaMa-2 on three tasks, navigate to the following link:

*https://www.anyscale.com/blog/fine-tuning-llama-2-a-comprehensive-case-study-for-tailoring-models-to-unique-applications*

## Fine Tuning LlaMa-2

Although LlaMa-2 is an improvement over its predecessor LlaMa, you can further improve the performance of Llama-2 by performing some fine tuning of this LLM.

*https://medium.com/@murtuza753/using-llama-2-0-faiss-and-langchain-for-question-answering-on-your-own-data-682241488476*

The following article shows you how to fine tune LlaMa-2 in a Google Colaboratory notebook:

*https://towardsdatascience.com/fine-tune-your-own-llama-2-model-in-a-colab-notebook-df9823a04a32*

The following article describes how to use MonsterAPI (also discussed in the article) in order to fine tune LlaMa-2 in five steps:

*https://blog.monsterapi.ai/how-to-fine-tune-llama-2-llm/*

The following link describes how to access LlaMa-2 in Google Colaboratory:

*https://levelup.gitconnected.com/harnessing-the-power-of-llama-2-using-google-colab-2e1dedc2d1d8*

## WHEN IS GPT-5 AVAILABLE?

As this book goes to print, there is no official information available regarding the status of GPT-5, which is to say that everything is speculative. In the early part of 2023 Sam Altman (CEO of OpenAI) remarked that there were "no official plans" for GPT-5.

However, during mid-2023 OpenAI filed a patent for GPT-5 in which there are some high-level details about the features of GPT-5. Some people have speculated that GPT-5 will be a more powerful version of GPT-4, and others suggest that filing a patent might be nothing more than securing the name GPT-5 by OpenAI.

Regardless of the motivation for filing a patent, there is a great deal of competition with GPT-4 from various companies. Therefore, it's highly plausible that OpenAI will release GPT-5, perhaps by the end of 2023. Regarding model sizes, recall that GPT-3 has 175B parameters, and some speculate that GPT-4 has 10 trillion parameters, which would mean that GPT-4 is roughly 60 times larger than GPT-3. The same increase in scale for GPT-5 seems implausible because GPT-5 would then consist of 600 trillion parameters.

Another possibility is that GPT-4 is based on the MoE (Mixture of Experts) methodology that involves multiple components. For instance, GPT-4 could be a combination of 8 components, each of which involves 220 million parameters, and therefore GPT-4 would consist of 1.76 trillion parameters.

Keep in mind that training LLMs such as GPT-4 is very costly and requires huge datasets for the pre-training step. Regardless of the eventual size of GPT-5, the training process could involve enormous costs.

## SUMMARY

This chapter started with a discussion of ChatGPT from OpenAI and some of its features. In addition, you will learn about some competitors to ChatGPT, such as Claude-2 from Anthropic.

Next, you learned about GPT-4 from OpenAI, which powers ChatGPT, and some of its features. Then you learned about some competitors of GPT-4, such as Llama-2 (Meta) and Bard (Google).

CHAPTER 6

# ChatGPT and Python Code

This chapter contains examples of using ChatGPT in order to perform an eclectic mix of `Python` tasks, from generating `Python` code for a simple calculator to generating code to calculate probabilities involved in throwing two or more dice.

Keep in mind that ChatGPT generated all the code samples in this chapter. Although the example of `asyncio` in Listing 6.10 executes with an error, ChatGPT provided debugging suggestions that eventually led to the successful execution of this code that is shown in Listing 6.11. The complete debugging "session" with ChatGPT is approximately three pages, and it's displayed in its entirety after Listing 6.10. Indeed, this code sample shows you the remarkable capability of ChatGPT.

One other comment: Chapter 5 provides details of ChatGPT and GPT-4, and if you prefer, you can read that chapter before reading this chapter, but it's not necessary in order for you to understand the material in this chapter.

The first part of this chapter starts with an example of generating a simple numeric calculator that you can extend by providing additional functionality (such as support for trigonometric functions). This section also contains `Python` code for handling text file and scraping Web sites.

The second part of this chapter contains `Python` code for creating a basic chatbot as well as performing data visualization. In addition, you will learn how to generate random numbers `Pandas`.

The third part of this chapter introduces you to Fibonacci numbers, OOP (object oriented programming), asynchronous programming, and how to work with the requests library in `Python`.

The fourth part of this chapter shows you how to use `PIL` for processing images, how to handle exceptions, as well as an introduction to generators and decorators in `Python`. The final section of this chapter shows you how to calculate the probability of obtaining a certain number when rolling two, three, or four fair dice.

## SIMPLE CALCULATOR

Listing 6.1 displays the contents of `simple_calculator.py` that ChatGPT generated as a rudimentary calculator.

***LISTING 6.1: simple_calculator.py***

```
def calculator(a, b, operation):
    if operation == 'add':
        return a + b
    elif operation == 'subtract':
        return a - b
    elif operation == 'multiply':
        return a * b
    elif operation == 'divide':
        if b == 0:
            return "Cannot divide by zero!"
        return a / b
    else:
        return "Invalid operation"

# Usage
result = calculator(5, 3, 'add')
print(result)  # Output: 8
```

Listing 6.1 starts with a `Python` function that processes two integers a and b and also an arithmetic operator. The code consists of a sequence of if/elif statements that add, subtract, multiply, or divide the numbers a and b, provided that the value of operator is add, subtract, multiple, and divide, respectively. If the operator is not in this list, then a message is returned to the main part of the program. The final portion of Listing 6.1 invokes the `calculate()` function with the numbers 3 and 5 and the operator add.

As you can see, there is no error checking in order to ensure that a and b are both numeric values, and there is no check for the operator to ensure that it always consists of lowercase letters. Launch the code in Listing 6.1 and you will see that its output is the value 8.

## SIMPLE FILE HANDLING

Listing 6.2 displays the contents of `file_handling.py` that ChatGPT generated in order to read content from a file and then write new content to a different file.

***LISTING 6.2: file_handling.py***

```
def read_file(file_path):
    with open(file_path, 'r') as file:
        return file.read()

def write_to_file(file_path, content):
    with open(file_path, 'w') as file:
        file.write(content)
```

```
# Usage
content = read_file('source.txt')
write_to_file('destination.txt', content)
```

Listing 6.2 starts with two `Python` functions `read_file()` and `write_to_file()` that read the contents of a file and write text to a file, respectively.

The function `read_file()` invokes the `open()` function in order to open a text file in read-only mode and then returns the contents of the file via the `file.read()` code snippet.

The function `write_to_file()` invokes the `open()` function in order to open a text file in write-only mode and then write the contents of content to the file. The final portion of Listing 6.2 invokes the `read_file()` function with the filename `source.txt` and then invokes the `write_to_file()` function with the contents of the file source.txt.

Notice several details about this code sample. First, there is no error handling to check if the path to the file `destination.txt` exists, or to handle the case where the path is valid but the file does not exist. Second, the code does not check if the file `destination.txt` has write privileges.

Create a file called source.txt and place some text in this file. Next, launch the code in Listing 6.2 and then confirm that `destination.txt` contains the same text as the file `source.txt`.

## SIMPLE WEB SCRAPING

Listing 6.3 displays the contents of `web_scraping.py` that ChatGPT generated to perform Web scraping. Make sure you have installed the libraries `BeautifulSoup` and requests, which you can perform from the command line as follows:

```
pip3 install bs4
pip3 install requests
```

***LISTING 6.3: web_scraping.py***

```
import requests
from bs4 import BeautifulSoup

def scrape_titles(url):
    response = requests.get(url)
    soup = BeautifulSoup(response.content, 'html.parser')

    titles = []
    for title in soup.find_all('h2', class_='article-title'):
        titles.append(title.text)

    return titles
```

```
# Usage
# titles = scrape_titles('https://dummywebsite.com/articles')
# print(titles)
```

Listing 6.3 starts by importing `requests` and `BeautifulSoup`, followed by the function `scrap_titles()` that scrapes the contents of a given URL. Specifically, this function initializes the variable `response` with the result of invoking the `get()` method with a given URL. Next, this function initializes the variable `soup` with the parsed contents of response.content.

The second part of this function contains a loop that iterates through all the <h2> HTML tags that also have a class attribute equal to `article-title`. For each such item, the text of the item is appended to the `Python` variable titles, which is initialized as an empty `Python` list. When the loop has completed the code returns the variable `titles`, which consists of titles listed in the Web site.

The final portion of Listing 6.3 initializes the variable titles with the result o invoking scrape_titles() with a fictions URL and then displays the result. Replace the fictions URL with a valid URL, uncomment the final code snippets, and then check the generated output.

## BASIC CHAT BOT

Listing 6.4 displays the contents of `basic_chatbot.py` that ChatGPT generated to perform Web scraping.

***LISTING 6.4: basic_chatbot.py***

```
from bs4 import BeautifulSoup


def chatbot_response(text):
    responses = {
        'hello': 'Hi there!',
        'how are you': 'I am fine, thank you!',
        'bye': 'Goodbye!',
    }

    return responses.get(text.lower(), 'I am sorry, I do
not understand that.')


# Usage
response = chatbot_response('Hello')
print(response)  # Output: Hi there!
```

Listing 6.4 starts by importing `BeautifulSoup`, followed by the function `chatbot_responses()` that initializes the variable `responses` as a `Python` dictionary. The final portion of this function issues a `return` statement that converts the variable text to lowercase, and then the value associated with this lowercase string in the responses dictionary. If the string is not found, then a disclaimer type of message is returned.

The final portion of Listing 6.4 invokes the function `chatbot_response()` with the string `Hello`, which is a key in the `responses` dictionary. Launch the code in Listing 6.4 and you will see the output `Hi there!`., which is the value associated with the key `Hello` in the `responses` dictionary.

## BASIC DATA VISUALIZATION

Listing 6.5 displays the contents of `basic_visualization.py` that ChatGPT generated to perform simple data visualization. For this task, you'll need to have the `matplotlib` library installed as follows:

```
pip3 install matplotlib
```

***LISTING 6.5: basic_visualization.py***

```
import matplotlib.pyplot as plt

def plot_graph(x, y, title, x_label, y_label):
    plt.plot(x, y)
    plt.title(title)
    plt.xlabel(x_label)
    plt.ylabel(y_label)
    plt.grid(True)
    plt.show()

# Usage
x = [1, 2, 3, 4, 5]
y = [2, 4, 1, 3, 5]
plot_graph(x, y, 'Sample Line Graph', 'X-Axis', 'Y-Axis')
```

Listing 6.5 starts starts by importing `matplotlib.pyplot`, followed by the function `plot_graph()` that plots a line graph with a grid background as well as labeled horizontal and vertical axes.

The next portion of Listing 6.5 initializes the Python lists x and y and passes them to the `plot_graph()` function, along with the strings `'Sample Line Graph'`, `'X-Axis'`, and `'Y-Axis'` for labels for the title, horizontal axis, and the vertical axis, respectively. Launch the code in Listing 6.5 and you will see the line graph in Figure 6.1.

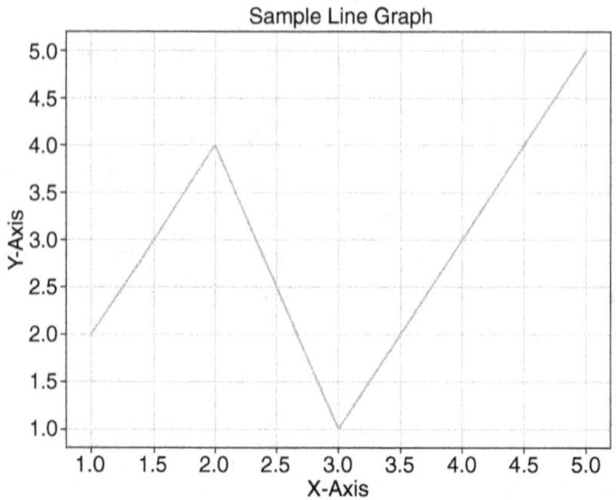


*FIGURE 6.1* A line graph rendered via Matplotlib.

## BASIC PANDAS

`Pandas` is a powerful library for data manipulation. Be sure to install `Pandas` via the following command from the command line:

```
pip3 install pandas
```

Listing 6.6 displays the contents of `basic_pandas.py` that ChatGPT generated to read the contents of a `CSV` file, and then compute the mean of a column in a subset of the rows of data.

### *LISTING 6.6: basic_pandas.py*

```
import matplotlib.pyplot as plt
import pandas as pd

def process_data(file_path):
    # Load data from CSV
    data = pd.read_csv(file_path)

    # Filter rows where 'value' column is greater than 50
    filtered_data = data[data['value'] > 50]

    # Compute the mean of the 'value' column
    mean_value = filtered_data['value'].mean()

    return mean_value

# Usage
mean = process_data('data.csv')
print('mean:',mean)
```

Listing 6.6 starts with two `import` statements, followed by the `process_data()` function that populates the variable `data`, which is a `Pandas` DataFrame, with the contents of a `CSV` file.

The next portion of this function initializes the variable `filtered_data` with the rows for which the `value` feature (attribute) is greater than 50. The final portion of this function invokes the `mean()` method on the rows in the variable `filtered_data` and then returns this value.

The final portion of Listing 6.6 invokes the function `process_data()` with the file `data.csv`. Create this file with some data of your choice, making sure that there is a column with the label `value`. Launch the code in Listing 6.6 and you will see the average of the rows in which `value` is greater than 50.

## GENERATE RANDOM DATA

Generate a list of random numbers and compute their mean and standard deviation. Listing 6.7 displays the contents of `random_data_stats.py` that ChatGPT generated to generate a set of random numbers and then display the contents of those numbers, as well as the mean and standard deviation of those numbers.

***LISTING 6.7: random_data_stats.py***

```
import random
import statistics

def generate_statistics(n):
    # Generate n random numbers between 1 and 100
    numbers = [random.randint(1, 100) for _ in range(n)]

    # Compute mean and standard deviation
    mean = statistics.mean(numbers)
    std_dev = statistics.stdev(numbers)

    return numbers, mean, std_dev

# Usage
numbers, mean, std_dev = generate_statistics(100)
print(f"Numbers: {numbers}")
print(f"Mean: {mean}")
print(f"Standard Deviation: {std_dev}")
```

Listing 6.7 starts with two `import` statements, followed by the `Python` function `generate_statistics()` that populates the `Python` list `numbers` with a set of n randomly generated integers that are between 1 and 100.

The next portion of this function invokes the methods `mean()` and `stdev()` of the `statistics` `Python` library in order to initialize the variables `mean` and `std_dev` with the mean and standard deviation, respectively, of the integers in `numbers`. The final code snippet in this function returns `numbers`, `mean`, and `std_dev`.

The final portion of Listing 6.7 initializes the variables `numbers`, `mean`, and `std_dev` with the result that is returned by invoking `generate_statistics()`

with the value 100 (which is the number of randomly generated numbers) and then displays their values. Launch the code in Listing 6.7 and you will see the following type of output (your output will be slightly different):

```
Numbers: [78, 41, 14, 67, 74, 90, 73, 2, 49, 22, 41, 86,
66, 62, 56, 73, 19, 38, 71, 8, 81, 38, 52, 80, 6, 52, 44,
48, 60, 87, 90, 43, 16, 46, 9, 65, 18, 22, 42, 45, 97, 19,
99, 17, 80, 47, 31, 12, 45, 35, 21, 26, 28, 88, 87, 93, 16,
19, 96, 16, 49, 29, 41, 25, 29, 39, 73, 45, 88, 17, 40, 5,
47, 29, 42, 71, 88, 93, 71, 89, 17, 96, 23, 92, 8, 71, 2,
56, 67, 87, 87, 38, 36, 51, 32, 89, 37, 59, 53, 86]
Mean: 50.43
Standard Deviation: 28.01127298323684
```

## RECURSION: FIBONACCI NUMBERS

The Fibonacci sequence is a classic example of a problem that can be solved using recursion. As you can see, each Fibonacci number is the sum of the two preceding Fibonacci numbers.

Listing 6.8 displays the contents of `fibonacci.py` that shows you how to compute the n-th Fibonacci number using recursion.

***LISTING 6.8: fibonacci.py***

```
def fibonacci(n):
    if n <= 1:
        return n
    return fibonacci(n-1) + fibonacci(n-2)

# Usage
result = fibonacci(10)
print(result)  # Output: 55
```

Listing 6.8 starts with the Python function `fibonacci()` that contains the standard type of code for calculating Fibonacci numbers recursively. Launch the code in Listing 6.8 and you will see the value 55 as the output.

## OBJECT-ORIENTED PROGRAMMING

Listing 6.9 displays the contents of `python_oop.py` that generates a rudimentary `Python` class that simulates two players who can score points.

***LISTING 6.9: python_oop.py***

```
class Player:
    def __init__(self, name):
        self.name = name
        self.score = 0

    def add_points(self, points):
        self.score += points
```

```
    def get_score(self):
        return self.score

# Usage
player = Player('Alice')
player.add_points(10)
print(f"{player.name}'s score: {player.get_score()}")
```

Listing 6.9 starts with the definition of the custom `Python` class `Player` that consists of three methods. The first method is the `__init__()` method that acts as a constructor in `Python`. This method initializes the `name` and `score` variables, which represent a player's `name` and `score`, respectively.

The second method is `add_points()` that increments a player's score with the value of the variable `points`. The third method is `get_score()` that returns the value of the current player's score.

The final portion of Listing 6.9 initializes the variable `player` as an instance of the `Player` class with the name `Alice`, which initializes name and score as Alice and 0, respectively. The next code snippet invokes `add_points()` to add 10 points to Alice's score, and then displays the name and score values. Launch the code in Listing 6.9 and you will see the following output.

```
Alice's score: 10
```

## ASYNCHRONOUS PROGRAMMING WITH ASYNCIO

This code sample demonstrates asynchronous programming by simulating two tasks running concurrently. Note that the first version of `async_example.py` executed with an error, which you will see later in this section. The good news is that ChatGPT provided several suggestions, one of which resulted in a successful execution of the code.

The complete "dialogue" with ChatGPT to fix the issue is approximately three pages in length, and it's displayed after the contents of Listing 6.10.

**NOTE** *This example is best suited for Python 3.7+.*

***LISTING 6.10: async_example.py***

```
import asyncio

async def task_one():
    await asyncio.sleep(2)
    print("Task One Completed!")

async def task_two():
    await asyncio.sleep(1)
    print("Task Two Completed!")

# Usage
asyncio.run(asyncio.gather(task_one(), task_two()))
```

Asynchronous programming lets us handle tasks concurrently. In this example, `task_two()` completes before `task_one()` because because the former has a the shorter sleep time than the latter, even though the latter is invoked before the former.

Listing 6.10 starts with an import statement, followed by the two functions `task_one()` and `task_two()` that are invoked asynchronously. These functions invoke the `asyncio.sleep()` method with the values 2 and 3, respectively, which is the number of seconds that these functions will sleep before resuming execution. Launch the code in Listing 6.10 and the following output was displayed:

```
Traceback (most recent call last):
  File "async_example.py", line 14, in <module>
    loop.run_until_completed(task_one(), task_two())
AttributeError: '_UnixSelectorEventLoop' object has no
attribute 'run_until_completed'
```

Since this code sample was generated by ChatGPT, here's the subsequent interaction with ChatGPT:

*ME: "I tried to execute your code sample and got an error [insert the error message]"*

```
ChatGPT:
This code seems correct. It defines two asynchronous
functions (task_one and task_two), and then uses asyncio.
run and asyncio.gather to run them concurrently.
The error message you provided, ValueError: a coroutine was
expected, got <_GatheringFuture pending>, typically occurs
when there's an issue related to not awaiting a coroutine
or misusing asyncio.gather(). However, based on the code
provided, I don't see these issues present.

To further assist, I have a few questions:

1. Are you using a version of Python that is 3.7 or
   newer? The asyncio.run() function was introduced in
   Python 3.7.
2. Is there any other code in async_example.py or another
   file that might be contributing to this error?
3. Are there any modifications or additions you made to the
   provided code before running it?

If the answer to the first question is "yes" and there are
no other modifications, the code should run without the
mentioned error. Otherwise, please provide additional
details so I can assist further.
```

*ME: The answer to question #1 is yes, the answer to question #2 is no, and the answer to question #3 is no.*

```
ChatGPT:
Thank you for clarifying. Given your responses, the
provided code should work correctly in a Python 3.7 or
newer environment without modifications.
```

However, the error you're encountering is perplexing since the code appears to be correct. Here are some steps we can take to troubleshoot:

Python Interpreter: Ensure that you're running the code with the correct Python interpreter. Sometimes, systems have multiple Python versions installed, and there might be a mismatch. You can check the Python version by running python --version or python3 --version in the terminal or command prompt.

Virtual Environment: If you're using a virtual environment, ensure that it's activated and using Python 3.7 or newer.

Reinstallation: Occasionally, there might be inconsistencies or issues with the installed Python libraries. You can try reinstalling asyncio using pip:
pip install --upgrade --force-reinstall asyncio

After reinstalling, try running the code again.

External Interferences: Ensure that there aren't other scripts or tools that might be interfering with the asyncio module. For example, some third-party libraries or tools might patch or modify the behavior of asyncio.

Code Execution: Try executing the code in a different environment, such as an online Python compiler or a different machine, to see if the error persists.

Minimal Reproduction: To isolate the issue, you can create a new Python script with only the provided code and run it to see if the error still occurs.
If after trying these steps the error persists, there might be a deeper issue related to the specific environment or system configuration. In that case, it would be helpful to have more detailed information about the environment, any error stack traces, or other relevant details to further diagnose the problem.

*ME: I re-installed asyncio but the same error occurs.*

ChatGPT:
I'm sorry to hear that the issue persists. Let's take a different approach to address it.

Given the error message you provided, it seems that somewhere in the execution, the event loop expects a coroutine but is getting a future object instead.

We can try using a different way to run the asynchronous tasks and see if it resolves the error:
We can try using a different way to run the asynchronous tasks and see if it resolves the error:
Explicitly Creating an Event Loop:
Instead of using asyncio.run(), we can try creating an event loop explicitly and then use it to run the tasks.

At this point ChatGPT provided two modified versions of the `Python` code in Listing 6.10, the first of which is shown in Listing 6.11. Since the code in Listing 6.11 did work correctly, the second modified version is not included.

***LISTING 6.11: async_example2.py***

```
import asyncio

async def task_one():
    await asyncio.sleep(2)
    print("Task One Completed!")

async def task_two():
    await asyncio.sleep(1)
    print("Task Two Completed!")

# Create an event loop
loop = asyncio.get_event_loop()

# Run tasks using the created loop
try:
    loop.run_until_complete(asyncio.gather(task_one(),
task_two()))
finally:
    loop.close()
```

Launch the code in Listing 6.11 by invoking the following command from the command line:

```
python3.7 async_example2.py
```

The following output is displayed, and there is a short pause before the second output line is shown:

```
Task Two Completed!
Task One Completed!
```

*ME: Solution #1 worked successfully! Thank you!*

```
ChatGPT:
You're welcome! I'm glad to hear that the first solution
worked successfully!

Using an explicit event loop can sometimes help bypass
issues or conflicts that might arise with the default
handling of asyncio.run().

If you have any more questions or need further assistance
with any other topic, feel free to ask. Happy coding!
```

## WORKING WITH REQUESTS IN PYTHON

The `requests` library provides an intuitive way to send HTTP requests. Here, we fetch data from a given API URL and extract a specific piece of information using the key.

Listing 6.12 shows you the contents of `requests_example.py` that demonstrates Web API Interaction using the `Python requests` library in order to fetch data from an API and extract specific information.

***LISTING 6.12: requests_example.py***

```
import requests

def fetch_api_data(api_url, key):
    response = requests.get(api_url)
    response.raise_for_status()
    data = response.json()
    return data.get(key, None)

# Usage
# replace the fictitious URL with a real URL:
# result = fetch_api_data('https://api.sampleendpoint.com/
data', 'desired_key')
# print(result)
```

Listing 6.12 starts with an `import` statement and then the `fetch_api()` function that retrieves the contents of the specified URL. This function invokes the `get()` method and then initializes the variable data with the JSON-formatted return string.

The next portion of Listing 6.12 initialed the variable `result` with the return value from invoking the function `fetch_api_data()`. Keep in mind that you must replace the fictitious URL with a valid URL and a legitimate value for `desired_key` before you can launch the code.

## IMAGE PROCESSING WITH PIL

The `Python` Imaging Library (PIL) allows for a vast array of image processing tasks. The code sample in this section performs several transformations on the file `sample3.png`.

Listing 6.13 shows you how to open an image, apply a grayscale filter, and save the result. In case you have not already done so, you need to install the Pillow library, a fork of PIL.

***LISTING 6.13: image_processing.py***

```
from PIL import Image, ImageFilter, ImageDraw

# Open an image
image_path = "sample3.png"
image = Image.open(image_path)

# 1. Convert the image to grayscale
grayscale_image = image.convert("L")
grayscale_image.show("Grayscale Image")

# 2. Apply a blur filter to the image
blurred_image = image.filter(ImageFilter.BLUR)
blurred_image.show("Blurred Image")

# 3. Rotate the image by 90 degrees
rotated_image = image.rotate(90)
rotated_image.show("Rotated Image")

# 4. Resize the image
new_dimensions = (300, 300)
resized_image = image.resize(new_dimensions)
resized_image.show("Resized Image")

# 5. Draw a red rectangle on the image
draw = ImageDraw.Draw(image)
draw.rectangle([(50, 50), (150, 150)], outline="red",
width=3)
image.show("Image with Rectangle")

# Save the processed images (optional)
grayscale_image.save("grayscale_output.jpg")
blurred_image.save("blurred_output.jpg")
rotated_image.save("rotated_output.jpg")
resized_image.save("resized_output.jpg")
image.save("rectangle_output.jpg")
```

Listing 6.13 starts with an import statement and then initializes the variable image with the result of invoking the `Image.open()` method with the file `sample3.png`. The next five code blocks apply transformations in order to generate 5 JPG files with the following names:

- `grayscale_output.jpg`
- `blurred_output.jpg`
- `rotated_output.jpg`
- `resized_output.jpg`
- `rectangle_output.jpg`

Launch the code in Listing 6.13 and you will see the preceding list of JPG files in your directory. Figure 6.2 displays the image that is generated by the first code block in Listing 6.13.

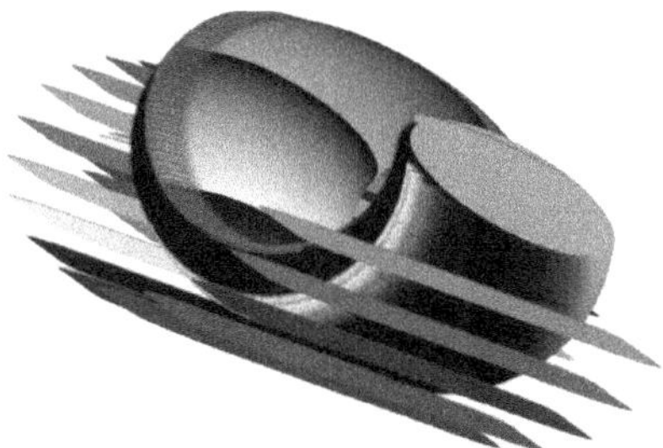

*FIGURE 6.2* A grayscale image.

Figure 6.3 displays the image that is generated by the second code block in Listing 6.13.

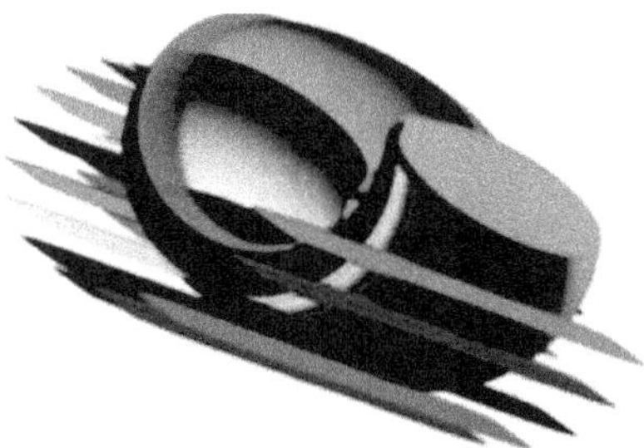

*FIGURE 6.3* A blurred image.

Figure 6.4 displays the image that is generated by the third code block in Listing 6.13.

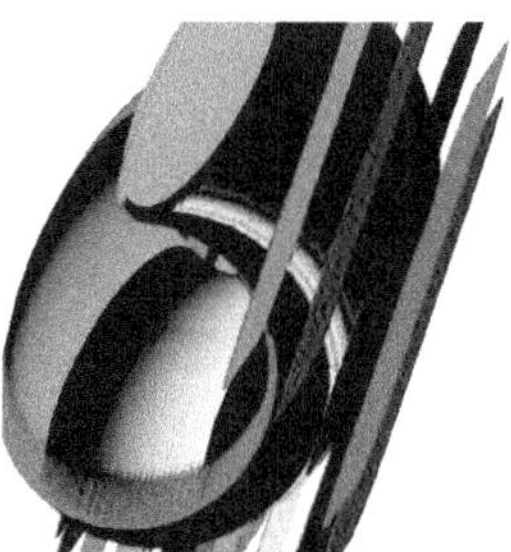

*FIGURE 6.4* A rotated image.

Figure 6.5 displays the image that is generated by the fourth code block in Listing 6.13.

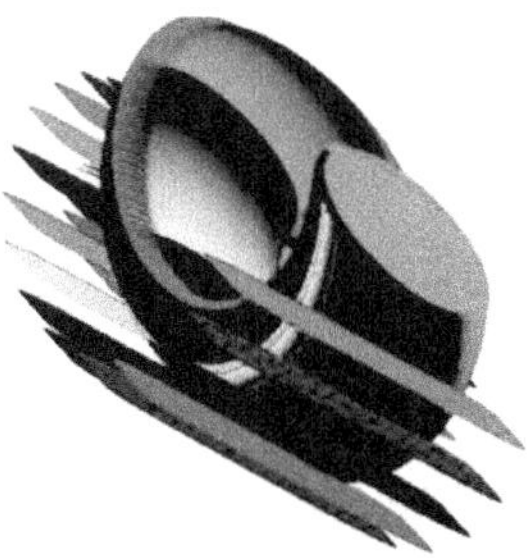

*FIGURE 6.5* A resized image.

Figure 6.6 displays the image that is generated by the fifth code block in Listing 6.13.

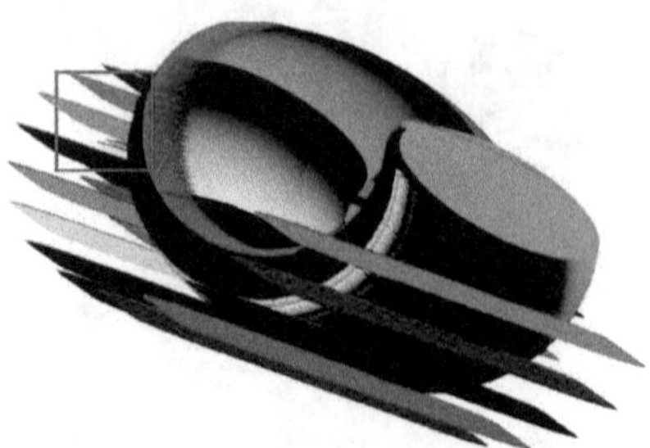

*FIGURE 6.6* A rectangular image.

Figure 6.7 displays the original image that Listing 6.13 uses in order to generate the preceding images.

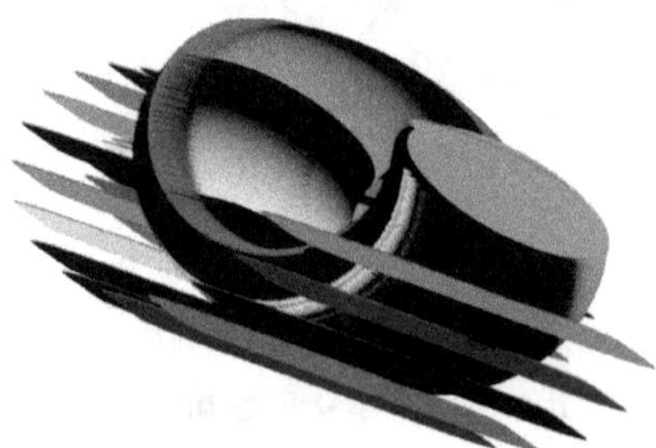

*FIGURE 6.7* The original image.

## EXCEPTION HANDLING

Exception handling is crucial for robust programs. In this example, we define a custom exception and showcase its usage and handling. Listing 6.14 shows you perform custom exception handling in `Python`.

***LISTING 6.14: exception_handling.py***

```
class CustomError(Exception):
    pass

def raise_custom_exception(condition):
    if condition:
        raise CustomError("This is a custom exception!")

try:
    raise_custom_exception(True)
except CustomError as ce:
    print(f"Caught an exception: {ce}")
```

Listing 6.14 starts with the definition of the `CustomError` class that extends the `Python Exception` class. This class contains the raise_custom_exception() function that simply raises an exception if the condition is true.

The second half of Listing 6.14 consists of a try/except block in which the custom exception is explicitly raised (a bit artificial, but it serves its purpose). The except portion of the code invokes print() to display a message. Launch the code in Listing 6.14 and you will see the following output.

```
Caught an exception: This is a custom exception!
```

## GENERATORS IN PYTHON

Generators allow for lazy evaluation, producing values on-the-fly without storing the entire sequence in memory. Listing 6.15 shows you the contents of fibonacci2.py that shows you how to define a generator that produces Fibonacci numbers in Python.

***LISTING 6.15: fibonacci2.py***

```
def fibonacci_generator(n):
    a, b = 0, 1
    for _ in range(n):
        yield a
        a, b = b, a + b

# Usage
for num in fibonacci_generator(10):
  print(num)
```

Listing 6.15 starts with the function fibonacci_generator() that is a Python generator because of the placement of the yield statement. The details of Python generators are outside the scope of this book, but you can find online resources that go into detail regarding Python generators.

The final portion of Listing 6.15 invokes the function fibonacci_generator() with the value 10 and then prints the returned value in a loop. Launch the code in Listing 6.15 and you will see the following output:

```
0
1
1
2
3
5
8
13
21
34
```

## ROLL 7 OR 11 WITH TWO DICE

This section contains a dialogue with ChatGPT to determine the probability of rolling a 7 or an 11 with two balanced dice.

*Me: Suppose that I toss two fair dice and I win if the sum of the values is either 7 or 11. What is the probability that I win and please provide an explanation.*

```
ChatGPT:
Alright, let's break this down step by step.
There are two dice, and each die has 6 faces. So, when you
roll two dice, there are a total of 6×6=366×6=36 possible
outcomes, as each die can land on any of its 6 sides
independently of the other.

Now, let's consider the ways to get a sum of 7:
    Die 1 shows 1, Die 2 shows 6.
    Die 1 shows 2, Die 2 shows 5.
    Die 1 shows 3, Die 2 shows 4.
    Die 1 shows 4, Die 2 shows 3.
    Die 1 shows 5, Die 2 shows 2.
    Die 1 shows 6, Die 2 shows 1.
That's 6 ways to get a sum of 7.

Next, let's consider the ways to get a sum of 11:
    Die 1 shows 5, Die 2 shows 6.
    Die 1 shows 6, Die 2 shows 5.
That's 2 ways to get a sum of 11.

Combining both possibilities, there are a total of
6+2=86+2=8 ways to win.

So, the probability P of winning is given by:
P = (Number of winning outcomes)/(Total possible outcomes)

Let's compute the probability.

Given the number of winning outcomes as 8 and the total
possible outcomes when tossing two dice as 36, the
probability PP of winning is:
P = 8/36 = 2/9

Thus, the probability of winning is 2/9 or approximately
0.2222 (rounded to four decimal places).

In summary, when you toss two fair dice, the probability
that the sum of their values is either 7 or 11 is 2/9.
```

## ROLL 7 OR 11 WITH THREE DICE

This section contains a dialogue with ChatGPT to determine the probability of rolling a 7 or an 11 with three balanced dice.

*Me: Suppose that I toss three fair dice and I win if the sum of the values is either 7 or 11. What is the probability that I win and please provide an explanation?*

ChatGPT:

When you roll three dice, each die can land on any of its 6 sides independently of the others. So, there are a total of 6×6×6=2166×6×6=216 possible outcomes.

Now, let's consider the ways to get a sum of 7 with three dice:

1, 1, 5
1, 2, 4
1, 3, 3
1, 4, 2
1, 5, 1
2, 1, 4
2, 2, 3
2, 3, 2
2, 4, 1
3, 1, 3
3, 2, 2
3, 3, 1
4, 1, 2
4, 2, 1
5, 1, 1

That's 15 ways to get a sum of 7 with three dice. Next, let's consider the ways to get a sum of 11:

2, 3, 6
2, 4, 5
2, 5, 4
2, 6, 3
3, 2, 6
3, 3, 5
3, 4, 4
3, 5, 3
3, 6, 2
4, 2, 5
4, 3, 4
4, 4, 3
4, 5, 2
5, 2, 4
5, 3, 3
5, 4, 2
6, 2, 3
6, 3, 2

That's 18 ways to get a sum of 11 with three dice. Combining both possibilities, there are a total of 15+18=3315+18=33 ways to win. So, the probability PP of winning is given by:

P = (Number of winning outcomes)/(Total possible outcomes)

Let's compute the probability. When you toss three fair dice, the probability that the sum of their values is either 7 or 11 is approximately 0.15280.1528 (rounded to four decimal places). To explain:

There are 15 possible combinations to get a sum of 7.

There are 18 possible combinations to get a sum of 11.

Combining both, there are 33 ways you can win out of a total of 216 possible outcomes. Therefore, the winning probability is 33/216 ≈ 0.152821633 ≈ 0.1528.

In summary, when you toss three dice, the probability of their values summing up to either 7 or 11 is about 15.28%.

## ROLL 7 OR 11 WITH FOUR DICE

This section contains a dialogue with ChatGPT to determine the probability of rolling a 7 or an 11 with four balanced dice.

*Me: Suppose that I toss three fair dice and I win if the sum of the values is either 7 or 11. What is the probability that I win and please provide an explanation.*

```
ChatGPT:
    When dealing with four dice, calculating the
probability of their sum equating to either 7 or 11
involves considering a lot more combinations than with
fewer dice. Let's tackle the problem step by step.
    When you roll four dice, each die can land on any of
its 6 sides independently of the others. So, the total
possible outcomes are 6×6×6×6=1,2966×6×6×6=1,296.
    To determine the number of winning outcomes (sums of 7
or 11), we'll enumerate the combinations for each case:
We'll start by calculating all the combinations that give a
sum of 7.
Then, we'll calculate all the combinations that give a sum
of 11.
Finally, we'll sum up the counts from both cases and divide
by the total possible outcomes to get the probability.
    This computation can be quite involved, so we'll use
a programmatic approach to enumerate all the possible
combinations and count the ones that result in sums of 7 or
11.
    When you toss four fair dice, the probability that the
sum of their values is either 7 or 11 is approximately
0.09570.0957 (rounded to four decimal places). To explain:
    There are several possible combinations of four dice
that can sum up to either 7 or 11.
    Out of the 64=1,29664=1,296 possible outcomes
when tossing four dice, there are a specific number of
combinations that result in a sum of either 7 or 11.
    Using a programmatic approach, we determined that the
number of such combinations relative to the total possible
outcomes yields a probability of about 9.57%.
    In summary, when you toss four dice, the probability of
their values summing up to either 7 or 11 is about 9.57%.
```

## MEAN AND STANDARD DEVIATION

Please calculate the mean and standard deviation of the numbers in the set S = {9, 2, –8, 17, 4, 37} and please provide details.

Listing 6.16 shows you the contents of `mean_std.py` that ChatGPT generated in order to calculate the mean and standard deviation of a set of numbers.

***LISTING 6.16: mean_std.py***

```
import numpy as np

# Given set of numbers
S = [9, 2, -8, 17, 4, 37]

# Calculate mean and standard deviation
mean_S = np.mean(S)
std_dev_S = np.std(S)

print("mean_S    =",mean_S)
print("std_dev_S =",std_dev_S)
```

Listing 6.16 starts with an `import` statement and then initializes the set `S` with six numbers. The next code snippets initialize the variables `mean_S` and `std_dev_S` by invoking the methods `mean()` and `std()`, respectively, of the `NumPy` library. The final portion of Listing 6.16 displays the values of these variables. Launch the code in Listing 6.16 and you will see the following output:

```
mean_S = np.mean(S)
mean_S    = 10.166666666666666
std_dev_S = 14.158821357098276
```

## SUMMARY

This chapter contains `Python`-based solutions generated by ChatGPT to a variety of tasks. The first set of tasks involved tasks such as creating a simple calculator, Web scraping, and file-based operations.

Then you learned about data visualization using a popular open source `Python`-based library called `Matplotlib`. In addition, you learned how to use recursion in order to calculate Fibonacci numbers, followed by an example that uses a generator to calculate Fibonacci numbers.

You also saw a very interesting example of how to interact with ChatGPT in order to debug a code sample that was generated by ChatGPT in Listing 6.10 and Listing 6.11.

In addition, you learned how to perform image processing in `Python` that involved multiple transformations on a PNG file. Moreover, you saw how to define custom exception handlers in `Python`, as well as how to work with generators in `Python`.

Moreover, you learned how to calculate probabilities of obtaining a given number by tossing 2, 3, or 4 well-balanced dice. Finally, you saw how to calculate the mean and the standard deviation of a set of numbers.

# Index

## M



## N



## O



## P

**Q**



**R**

www.ingramcontent.com/pod-product-compliance
Lightning Source LLC
LaVergne TN
LVHW050635100826
845148LV00011B/1876

* 9 7 8 1 5 0 1 5 2 2 2 8 4 *